CAPTIVATING

UNVEILING THE MYSTERY OF A WOMAN'S SOUL

UPDATED EDITION

STUDY GUIDE | SIX SESSIONS

JOHN & STASI ELDREDGE

WITH ALLEN ARNOLD

Captivating Study Guide (Updated Edition)

Published by HarperChristian Resources, 3950 Sparks Drive SE, Suite 101, Grand Rapids, MI 49546, USA. HarperChristian Resources is a registered trademark of HarperCollins Christian Publishing, Inc.

Requests for information should be addressed to customercare@harpercollins.com.

ISBN 978-0-310-18391-4 (softcover)
ISBN 978-0-310-18392-1 (ebook)

HarperChristian Resources titles may be purchased in bulk for church, business, fundraising, or ministry use. For information, please email ResourceSpecialist@ChurchSource.com.

Published in association with Yates & Yates, LLP, Literary Agents, Orange, California.

HarperCollins Publishers, Macken House, 39/40 Mayor Street Upper, Dublin 1, D01 C9W8, Ireland (https://www.harpercollins.com).

Art direction: Ron Huizinga
Cover Design: Samson Creative

First Printing April 2026 / Printed in the United States of America

CONTENTS

INTRODUCTION

INTRO

I have always wanted to read a novel or enjoy a movie where the heroine was a normal, average-looking woman with an ordinary life who was not a concert pianist, brain surgeon, underwear model, or superhero in her spare time. I want to read about a woman like me. A woman like you. And I want to learn from her. In choosing to do this study—by yourself, or better still, with a group of women—you are getting that opportunity! You will learn from the stories of women like yourself, and women not so like you. If you are doing this in a group, covenant together to make this a place of safety and confidentiality, a place where each woman is quick to listen and slow to offer advice. (Receiving advice often feels like people trying to fix us . . . when all we really long for is to be understood.) But whether you are working through this in a group or alone, take your time! Journal through the questions. After all, this is for you.

We women share so much. We have much more in common than most of us realize. It's true. For one thing, we live with the mystery of hormones. Often, just when it seems we begin to get them figured out, they change on us. Most of us love to shop and all of us love a bargain. We don't so much like our hair, and we really don't like our annual appointment. (You know the one.) We love a good story and we love certain smells, and we love to go to the bathroom in groups.

And then there's the other side to us . . . the deeper side. There are times when we wake in the middle of the night to sorrow, loneliness, and an ache for something more that largely goes unexplained. We stop at red lights and while we wait, the ache rises to the surface again—ignoring our efforts to shame ourselves into wanting less. We are women. We think no one really understands. We tend to believe there is something deeply wrong with us. We think that if we were better somehow, then life wouldn't be so hard, painful, lonely, fill in the blank.

But what if the ache is a gift?

What if God is calling to us through the cry of our hearts that urges us to reach for that "something more" we all long for? What if the truest thing about us is that we are magnificent and meant to be the heroine of the story? Really.

Let's risk taking a look at the "what if." Come, journey with me into a realm of wonder and possibility, beauty, and hope . . . into the very heart of a woman.

Stasi

SESSION ONE

THE HEART OF A WOMAN

GROUP STUDY

"Sometimes it's hard to be a woman."

—Tammy Wynette

Welcome!

Welcome to Session One of *Captivating*. If this is your first time together as a group or there are new members in your group, take a moment to introduce yourselves to one another before watching the video. We suggest you simply share your name, some brief details about your life, and what has moved you to join this study. Then, let's get started!

Core Scripture

Look up Proverbs 4:23 and write it in the space below.

Invite several women to read various translations of the passage aloud. Listen for fresh insights and share any thoughts about this verse with the group.

VIDEO

Watch the video segment for Session One, streaming or on DVD. This study guide includes free streaming access to all six videos. Instructions are located on the inside front cover of the guide. The summary is provided for your benefit as well as space to take additional notes as you watch.

Summary

This is a study of discovery. A journey, really. For you to discover who God meant when he meant you.

What does it mean to be a woman? What is my calling in life? What does God value? What does He want from me? What do I want? And is that okay?

We are not carbon copies of each other. Not at all. God loves diversity and he has fashioned each one of us uniquely and well. But it is a very good thing to know that we are not alone on this journey of life; we have much more in common with each other—simply because we are women—than we don't. We share more than most of us realize.

For instance, we have a feminine heart. We have to start there, because as the Scriptures tell us, the heart is the center of it all.

Think about it: God created you as a woman. "God created man in his own image . . . male and female he created them" (Genesis 1:27). Whatever it means to bear God's image, you do so as a woman. Female. That's how and where you bear his image. And not in your body. The Trinity does not have a body. No, you bear God's image in your heart.

Your feminine heart has been created with the greatest of all possible dignities—as a reflection of God's own heart. You are a woman to your soul, to the very core of your being. And so the journey to discover what God meant when he created woman in his image—when he created you as his woman—that journey begins with your heart. Another way of saying this is that the journey begins with desire.

The stories we love reveal much of the secret desires of our deep hearts. If you take a close look, talk with the women in your life, you'll find that we share themes in our core desires. They are not all that we want and they play out differently in our lives, but in her heart of hearts, every woman longs to be romanced, to play an irreplaceable role in a heroic adventure and to unveil beauty.

It is right that we do, for it is in these desires that we bear the image of our God.

GROUP DISCUSSION

Choose the questions that work best for your group.

1. Could you relate to the stories and struggles the women shared with each other? Why or why not?

2. What was evoked for you during this session? Did it surprise you? Share your initial thoughts briefly with one another.

3. Stasi says that your heart is the most important thing about you. Is this a new thought to you? What is your response to that statement?

4. How has your heart been valued in your life? Have you valued it as the treasure it is?

5. Which of the three core longings of a woman's heart do you struggle with most? What is it about that one that you push against?

6. Name one of your favorite movies or stories below. How does it highlight the core longings of a woman's heart?

7. In what area do you feel you've most lost heart? Do you feel it is possible to get it back? Why or why not?

Closing Prayer

Leader or volunteer, close your group time in prayer:

> *Dearest Father,*
> *I consecrate this book and this study to your Kingdom and Your purposes in my life. I want my whole heart back, Jesus. I want to be a woman who loves You with all of it. I give you permission to come for me in the places I need you to. Reveal to me more of who you really are and who I really am to you. I want to know you more deeply and love you more truly. Come for me. Instruct me. Guide me. Awaken me. Thank you, God. Thank you. In Jesus' Name. Amen.*

Recommended Reading

Before your group gathers for the next session, read Chapter 2 (*Created Eve / Fallen Eve*) in the book *Captivating*. Use the space provided to write any key points or questions you want to bring to the next group meeting.

BETWEEN-SESSIONS PERSONAL STUDY

In this section, you're invited to further explore the material we've covered this week from *Captivating*. Each day offers a short reading from Chapter 1 of John and Stasi's book—along with reflection questions designed to take you deeper into the themes of this week's study.

Journal or just jot a few thoughts after each question. At the start of the next session, there will be a few minutes to share any insights . . . but the primary goal of these questions is for your personal growth and private reflection.

UNSEEN, UNSOUGHT, AND UNCERTAIN

I know I am not alone in this nagging sense of failing to measure up, a feeling of not being good enough as *a woman*. Every woman I've ever met feels it—something deeper than just the sense of failing at what she does. An underlying, gut feeling of failing at who she is. *I am not enough*, and *I am too much* at the same time. Not pretty enough, not thin enough, not kind enough, not gracious enough, not disciplined enough. But too emotional, too needy, too sensitive, too strong, too opinionated, too messy. The result is *shame*, the universal companion of women. It haunts us, nipping at our heels, feeding on our deepest fear that we will end up abandoned and alone.

After all, if we were better women—whatever *that* means—life wouldn't be so hard. Right? We wouldn't have so many struggles; there would be less sorrow in our hearts. Why is it so hard to create meaningful friendships and sustain them? Why do our days seem so unimportant, filled not with romance and adventure but with duties and demands? We feel *unseen*, even by those who are closest to us. We feel *unsought*—that no one has the passion or the courage to pursue us, to get past our messiness to find the woman deep inside. And we feel uncertain—*uncertain* what it even means to be a woman; uncertain what it truly means to be feminine; uncertain if we are or ever will be.

Aware of our deep failings, we pour contempt on our own hearts for wanting more. Oh, we long for intimacy and for adventure; we long to be the Beauty of some great story. But the desires set deep in our hearts seem like a luxury, granted only to those women who get their acts together. The message to the rest of us—whether from a driven culture or a driven church—is "try harder."

In what areas of your life do you feel you aren't coming through or failing to measure up?

- Have you realized that other women feel this same way? Does this change your view that you're the only one missing the mark?

- Does it feel like the message of "try harder" is coming from God? What do you *honestly* believe God thinks about you right now, right in the middle of the messiness of your life?

DAY 2

A LOSS OF HEART

In all the exhortations we have missed the most important thing of all. We have missed the *heart* of a woman.

And that is not a wise thing to do, for as the Scriptures tell us, the heart is central. "Above all else, guard your heart, for it is the wellspring of life" (Prov. 4:23). Above all else. Why? Because God knows that our heart is core to who we are. It is the source of all our creativity, our courage, and our convictions. It is the fountainhead of our faith, our hope, and of course, our love. This "wellspring of life" within us is the very essence of our existence, the center of our being. Your heart as a woman is the most important thing about you.

Think about it: God created you *as a woman*. "God created man in his own image . . . male and female he created them" (Gen. 1:27). Whatever it means to bear God's image, you do so as a woman. Female. That's how and where you bear his image. Your feminine heart has been created with the greatest of all possible dignities—as a reflection of God's own heart. You are a woman to your soul, to the very core of your being. And so the journey to discover what God meant when he created woman in his image—when he created you as his woman—that journey begins with your heart. Another way of saying this is that the journey begins with *desire*. The desires that God has placed into our hearts are clues as to who we really are and the role that we are meant to play. Many of us have come to despise our desires or at least try to bury them. They have become a source of pain or shame. We are embarrassed of them. But we don't need to be. The desires of our heart bear a great glory because, as we will detail further in the next chapter, they are precisely where we bear the image of God. We long for certain things because *he* does!

- Based on your life experiences, do you agree that your heart as a woman is the most important thing about you (Proverbs 4:23)? Why or why not?

- How do you handle your heart when your core desires aren't being met? Why?

- What do you think it means to bear God's image as a woman?

DAY 3

TO BE ROMANCED

Look at the games that little girls play, and if you can, remember what you dreamed of as a little girl. Look at the movies women love. Listen to your own heart and the hearts of the women you know. What is it that a woman wants? What does she dream of? Think again of women like Tamar, Ruth, Rahab—not very "churchy" women, but women held up for esteem in the Bible. We think you'll find that every woman in her heart of hearts longs for three things: to be romanced, to play an irreplaceable role in a great adventure, and to unveil beauty. That's what makes a woman come alive.

One of my favorite games growing up was "kidnapped and rescued." I know many little girls who played this—or wished they had. To be the beauty, abducted by the bad guys, fought for and rescued by a hero—some version of this had a place in all our dreams. Like Sleeping Beauty, like Cinderella, like Maid Marian, or like Cora in *The Last of the Mohicans*, I wanted to be the heroine and have my hero come for me. Why am I embarrassed to tell you this? I simply loved feeling wanted and fought for. This desire is set deep in the heart of every little girl—and every woman. Yet most of us are ashamed of it. We downplay it. We pretend that it is less than it is. We are women of the twenty-first century after all—strong, independent, and capable, thank you very much. Uh-huh . . . and who is buying all those romance novels?

Think about the movies you once loved and the movies you love now. It is only recently that there are movies for little girls that don't have a handsome prince coming to rescue his beloved. Yet, *Sleeping Beauty*, *Snow White*, *Cinderella* and stories like them all speak to a little girl's longing for romance. She wants to be seen and desired, to be sought after and fought for. So the Beast must win Beauty's heart in *Beauty and the Beast*. So Mr. Darcy must walk across the field at dawn to proclaim his love to Miss Elizabeth in *Pride and Prejudice*. And we sigh.

Isn't something stirred in you when Matthew finally asks Mary to marry him as the snow begins to fall outside Downton Abbey or when Edward, *finally*, returns at the end of *Sense and Sensibility* to proclaim his love for Elinor? "Then . . . you're not . . . not married?" she asks, nearly holding her breath. "No," he says. "My heart is . . . and always will be . . . yours." Or how about when Jackson sings Shallows with Ally in *A Star is Born*? Or the sunset scene at the bow of the *Titanic*?

When we are young, we want to be precious to someone—especially Daddy. As we grow older, the desire matures into a longing to be pursued, desired, wanted as a woman. "Why am I so embarrassed by the depth of my desire for this?" asked a young friend just the other day. We were talking about her life as a single woman, and how she loves her work but would also like to be married. "I don't want to hang my life on it, but still, I yearn." Of course. You're a woman. You are made for relationship.

Now, being romanced isn't all that a woman wants, and John and I are certainly not saying that a woman ought to derive the meaning of her existence from whether or not she is being or has been romanced by a man . . . but don't you see that you want this? To be desired, to be pursued by one who loves you, to be someone's priority? Most of our addictions as women flare up when we feel that we are not loved or sought after. At some core place, maybe deep within, perhaps hidden or buried in her heart, every woman wants to be seen, wanted, and pursued. We want to be romanced.

- In your own words, how would you describe the desire to be romanced?

- Do you remember some of the games you played as a little girl? Which ones did you enjoy most . . . and why?

- Are you aware of your longing to be someone's priority? What does that look like for you?

DAY 4

AN IRREPLACEABLE ROLE IN A GREAT ADVENTURE

When I was a little girl, I used to love World War II movies. I imagined myself being in them. I dreamed of growing up, braiding my hair, and then tucking it up under my helmet. I planned to disguise my gender so that I could join in. Back in those days, women were not allowed to fight, I sensed that the men in these movies were part of something heroic, valiant, and worthy. I longed to be a part of it too. In the depths of my soul, I longed to be a part of something large and good; something that required all of me; something dangerous and worth dying for.

There is something fierce in the heart of a woman. Simply insult her man, or her best friend and you'll get a taste of it. Insult her children at your own peril. A woman is a warrior too. But she is meant to be a warrior in a uniquely feminine way. Sometime before the sorrows of life did their best to kill it in us, most young women wanted to be a part of something grand, something important. Before doubt and accusation take hold, most little girls sense that they have a vital role to play; they want to believe there is something in them that is needed and needed desperately.

Think of Sarah from *Sarah, Plain and Tall.* A man and his young children need her; their world is not right until she becomes a part of it. She brings her courage and her creativity to the West and helps to tame it. We are awed by the nurses in *Pearl Harbor*, how in the midst of a horrifying assault they bring their courage and strength to rescue the lives of hundreds of men. The women in The Lord of the Rings trilogy are valiant and beautiful—women like Arwen, Galadriel, and Éowyn change the fate of Middle Earth. And what about women like Esther, Deborah, Mary and Ruth? They were biblical characters who had irreplaceable roles in a Great Story. Not "safe" and "nice" women, not merely "sweet," but passionate and powerful women who were beautiful *as* warriors.

Why do I love remembering the story of canoeing in the dark beauty of the Tetons so much? Because I was needed. I was needed. Not only was I needed, but like Arwen, I was irreplaceable. No one else in that canoe could have done what I did.

Women love adventures of all sorts. Whether it be the adventure of horses (most girls go through a horse stage) or white-water rafting, going to a foreign country, performing onstage, climbing mountains, having children, starting a business, or diving ever more deeply into the heart of God, we were made to be a part of a great adventure. An adventure that is *shared*. We do not want the adventure merely for adventure's sake but for what it requires of us *for* others. We don't want to be alone in it; we want to be in it *with* others.

Sometimes the idea of living as a hermit appeals to all of us. No demands, no needs, no pain, no disappointments. But that is because we have been hurt, are worn out. In our heart of hearts, that place where we are most *ourselves*, we don't want to run away for very long. Our lives were meant to be lived with others. As echoes of the Trinity, we remember something. Made in the image of a perfect relationship, we are relational to the core of our beings and filled with a desire for transcendent purpose. We long to be an irreplaceable part of a shared adventure.

- What were your dreams for your life when you were a little girl? What did you want to be or do?

- Allow yourself to dream a little bit here. If you could do or be anything you wanted now, what would it be . . . and why?

- How would your living that life impact others? How is the life you are living now impacting others?

DAY 5
BEAUTY TO UNVEIL

Lovely little six-year-old Lacey was visiting our ministry outpost the other day, going from office to office, swinging on the doorframe, and asking with a smile, "Would you like to hear my song?" Her faced kissed by the sun with charming freckles, two front teeth missing, and eyes dancing with merriment, who could refuse her? She didn't really care if she was an interruption. I doubt the thought crossed her mind. She sang her newly made-up song about puppies and kitties, fully expecting to be delighted in, then skipped down the hall to grace the occupant of the next office. She was like a ray of summer sun or, better, a garden fairy, flitting from office to office. She was a little girl in her glory, unashamed in her desire to delight and be delighted in.

This desire to be beautiful is an ageless longing. My friend Lilly is in her mid-eighties. As she descended the stairs of her home one Christmas season, I was captured by her beauty. She was wearing a green corduroy jumper with a white turtleneck that had little candy canes all over it. I said, "Lilly, you look lovely!" Her face lit up, wrinkles and age spots disappearing as she put her hands out at her sides like a ballerina and did a delightful little twirl. She was no longer eighty—she was ageless. God has set eternity in our hearts. The longing to be beautiful is set there as well.

Now, we know that the desire to be beautiful has caused many women untold grief (how many diets have you been on?). Countless tears have been shed and hearts broken in its pursuit. Beauty has been extolled and worshiped and kept just out of reach for most of us. (Do you like having your picture taken? Do you like *seeing* those pictures later? How do you feel when people ask you your age? This issue of beauty runs deep!) For others, beauty has been shamed, used, and abused. Some of you have learned that possessing beauty can be dangerous. And yet—and this is just astounding—*in spite of* all the pain and distress that beauty has caused us as women, the desire remains.

During the midst of a talk I gave on the heart of a woman, one of the women in the audience leaned over to a friend and said, "I don't know what this whole thing is about—twirling skirts and all." The words had barely left her mouth when she burst into tears and had to leave the room. Little did she know how deep the desire ran, and how much pain it had caused. Many of us have hardened our hearts to this desire, the desire to be the Beauty. We, too, have been hurt so deeply in this area that we no longer identify with, perhaps even resent, the longing. But it's there.

And here is the important part - it's *not* just the desire for an outward beauty, but more—a desire to be captivating in the depths of *who you are.* An external beauty without a depth of character is not true beauty at all. As the Proverb says, "Like a gold ring in a pig's snout is a beautiful woman who shows no discretion" (11:22). Cinderella is beautiful, yes, but she is also good. Her outward beauty would be hollow were it not for the beauty of her heart. That's why we love her. In *The Sound of Music,* the countess has Maria beat in the looks department, and they both know it. But Maria has a rare and beautiful depth of spirit. She has the capacity to love snowflakes on kittens and mean-spirited children. She sees the handiwork of God in music and laughter and climbing trees. Her soul is *Alive.* And we are drawn to her.

- Who is beautiful to you . . . and why?

- What do you think it means to be beautiful on the inside? Is that of greater or lesser importance to you than being what the world defines as beautiful on the outside?

- What does the desire for a beauty to unveil look like for you?

CLOSING THOUGHTS

Well done, you. These were not easy questions to consider but I promise you it was time well spent. It was time spent honoring your own heart and life. This study is for you—for your heart—and for the goodness that God has for you by walking with him into the deeper regions hidden there. There are treasures to be found. Sometimes finding treasure is an easy affair and sometimes it requires a diligent search. In the days ahead, ask God to walk with you and guide you to discover every treasure that he has for you to possess. Though some chapters ahead may be stretching or perhaps even difficult, stay with it. The recovery of your heart is worth it. It's going to be good.

SESSION TWO

FALLEN EVE

GROUP STUDY

"Even to see her walk across the room is a liberal education."

—C.S. Lewis

Welcome!

Welcome to Session Two of *Captivating*. If there are new members in your group, take a moment to introduce yourselves to one another before watching the video.

If something stood out to you in your personal study, share briefly with your group.

Then, let's get started!

Core Scripture

Look up Genesis 2:18 and write it in the space below.

Invite several women to read various translations of the passage aloud. Listen for fresh insights and share any thoughts about this verse with the group.

VIDEO

Watch the video segment for Session Two, streaming or on DVD. This summary is provided for your benefit as well as space to take additional notes.

Summary

The story of creation is a wondrous and beautiful thing. Sometimes we forget that our story, the human story, begins with glory and beauty and goodness. In Genesis 1 we read the account of God setting his own image on the earth.

The LORD God formed the man from the dust of the ground and breathed into his nostrils the breath of life, and the man became a living being. (Gen. 2:7)

It is nearing the end of the sixth day, the end of the Creator's great labor, as Adam steps forth, the image of God, the triumph of his work. He alone is pronounced the son of God. And yet, the Master says that something is not good, not right. Something is missing . . . and that something is Eve.

The LORD God caused the man to fall into a deep sleep; and while he was sleeping, he took one of the man's ribs and then closed up the place with flesh. Then the LORD God made a woman from the rib[b] he had taken out of the man, and he brought her to the man. (Gen. 2:21–23)

She is the crescendo, the final, astonishing work of God. Woman. In one last flourish creation comes to a finish not with Adam, but with Eve. She is the Master's finishing touch. Eve is . . . breathtaking.

Woman wasn't created as an afterthought but as the pinnacle of creation.

If only the story could have stayed there. But it didn't. In this session, we will explore the fall of Eve . . . and how that impacts each of us today.

GROUP DISCUSSION

Choose the questions that work best for your group.

1. What about Jamie's story most stood out to you? Why?

2. What was evoked for you during this session? Was it new or calling up something buried in your heart?

3. How does the idea that women are the Crown of Creation sit with you?

4. The feeling that we need to hide our true selves has been around since the Garden of Eden. Added to our sense of not quite measuring up, there are times when the world has not been kind to us. Can you describe a time that you were hurt as a girl and it led you to hide your true self?

5. What current situations cause you to want to self-protect and hide? How do you do that?

6. What are you afraid will be exposed in these moments where you feel the need to hide?

7. Where would you like to know the love of God more deeply? How might doing so change your life?

Closing Prayer

Leader or volunteer, close your group time in prayer:

> *Dearest Father,*
> *Thank you that You have created me with dignity and honor. I am awed that you formed me in your own image. I know that there remain places in me where I need to know your love more deeply, places where I continue to hide and places I continue to go for soothing and comfort outside of your love. I ask for your help, God. Overwhelm me with the revelation of your love and strengthen me with courage to walk away from the ways I live out of fear. In Jesus' Name, I pray. Amen.*

Recommended Reading

Before your group gathers for the next session, read Chapters 4 (*Wounded)* and 6 *(Healing the Wound*) in the book *Captivating*. Use the space provided to write any key points or questions you want to bring to the next group meeting.

BETWEEN-SESSIONS PERSONAL STUDY

In this section, you're invited to further explore the material we've covered this week from *Captivating*. Each day offers a short reading from Chapter 2 (*What Eve Alone Can Tell*) or Chapter 3 (*Haunted by a Question*) of John and Stasi's book—along with reflection questions designed to take you deeper into the themes of this week's study.

Journal or just jot a few thoughts after each question. At the start of the next session, there will be a few minutes to share any insights . . . but the primary goal of these questions is for your personal growth and private reflection.

THE CROWN OF CREATION

Creation in its early stages begins like any great work of art—with uncut stone or a mass of clay, a rough sketch, a blank sheet of music. "Formless and empty" as Genesis 1:2 has it. Then God begins to fashion the raw materials he has made, like an artist working with the stone or sketch or page before him. Light and dark, heaven and earth, land and sea—it's beginning to take shape. With passion and brilliance the Creator works in large, sweeping movements on a grand scale. Great realms are distinguished from one another and established. Then he moves back over them again for a second pass as he begins to fill in color, detail, finer lines.

Forest and meadow burst forth. Tulips and pine trees and moss-covered stones. And notice—the masterpiece is becoming more intricate, more intimate.

From water and stone, to pomegranate and rose, to leopard and nightingale, creation *ascends* in beauty. The plot is thickening; the symphony is building and swelling, higher and higher to a crescendo. No wonder "the morning stars sang together and all the angels shouted for joy" (Job 38:7). A great hurrah goes up from the heavens. The greatest of all masterpieces is emerging. What was once formless and empty is now overflowing with life and color and sound and movement in a thousand variations. Most importantly, notice that each creature is *more* intricate and noble and mysterious than the last. A cricket is amazing, but it cannot compare to a wild horse.

Then something truly astonishing takes place.

God sets his own image on the earth. He creates a being like himself. He creates a son.

The LORD God formed the man from the dust of the ground and breathed into his nostrils the breath of life, and the man became a living being. (Gen. 2:7)

It is nearing the end of the sixth day, the end of the Creator's great labor, as Adam steps forth, the image of God, the triumph of his work. He alone is pronounced the son of God. Nothing in creation even comes close. Picture Michelangelo's *David*. He is . . . magnificent. Truly, the masterpiece seems complete. And yet, the Master says that something is not good, not right. Something is missing . . . and that something is Eve.

The LORD God caused the man to fall into a deep sleep; and while he was sleeping, he took one of the man's ribs and then closed up the place with flesh. Then the LORD God made a woman from the rib he had taken out of the man, and he brought her to the man. (Gen. 2:21–23)

She is the crescendo, the final, astonishing work of God. Woman. In one last flourish creation comes to a finish with *Eve*. She is the Master's finishing touch. How we wish this were an illustrated book, and we could show you now some painting or sculpture that captures this, like the stunning Greek sculpture of the goddess Nike of Samothrace, the winged beauty, just alighting on the prow of a great ship, her beautiful form revealed through the thin veils that sweep around her. Eve is . . . breathtaking.

Given the way creation unfolds, how it builds to ever higher and higher works of art, can there be any doubt that Eve is the crown of creation? Not an afterthought. Not a nice addition like an ornament on a tree. She is God's final touch, his pièce de résistance. She fills a place in the world nothing and no one else can fill. Step to a window, ladies, if you can. Better still, find some place with a view. Look out across the earth and say to yourselves, "The whole, vast world was incomplete without me. Creation reached its finishing touch in me."

- What does God's purposeful progression of creation reveal to you about your significance?

- Let's take another stab at it. Would it be possible that God saved the best for last and that being the final touch of creation holds a specific honor?

- Are there times or places in your life where believing that as a woman who bears the image of God, there is an untouchable honor to your life would have an impact? If so, where and how?

- Take a moment, look at something beautiful in nature and say to yourself, "The whole, vast world is incomplete without me. Creation reached its zenith in me." Breathe in that reality.

DAY 2
LIFESAVER

While Eve has a glory for relationship, that is not all she is essential for. Back in Genesis, when God sets his image bearers on the earth, he gives them their mission:

> And God blessed them, and God said to them, "Be fruitful and multiply and fill the earth and conquer it, and hold sway over the fish of the sea and the fowl of the heavens and every beast that crawls upon the earth." (Gen. 1:26–28 ALTER)

Call it the Human Mission—to be all and do all God sent us here to do. And notice—the mission to be fruitful and conquer and hold sway is given both to

Adam and to Eve. "And God said to them . . ." Eve is standing right there when God gives the world over to us. She has a vital role to play; she is a partner in this great adventure. All that human beings were intended to do here on earth—all the creativity and exploration, all the battle and rescue and nurture—we were intended to do together. In fact, not only is Eve needed, but she is desperately needed.

When God creates Eve, he calls her an ezer kenegdo. "It is not good for the man to be alone, I shall make him [an ezer kenegdo]" (Gen. 2:18 ALTER). Hebrew scholar Robert Alter, who has spent years translating the book of Genesis, says that this phrase is "notoriously difficult to translate." The various attempts we have in English are "helper" or "companion" or the notorious "help meet." Why are these translations so incredibly wimpy, boring, flat . . . disappointing? What is a help meet, anyway? What little girl dances through the house singing, "One day I shall be a help meet"? Companion? A dog can be a companion. Helper? Sounds like Hamburger Helper. Alter is getting close when he translates it "sustainer beside him."

The word *ezer* is used only twenty other places in the entire Old Testament. And in every other instance the person being described is God himself, when you need him to come through for you desperately.

There is no one like the God of Jeshurun, who rides on the heavens to help you . . .

> Blessed are you, O Israel! Who is like you, a people saved by the LORD? He is your shield and *helper* and your glorious sword. (Deut. 33:26, 29, emphasis added)

> I lift up my eyes to the hills—where does my *help* come from? My help comes from the LORD, the Maker of heaven and earth. (Ps. 121:1–2, emphasis added)

> May the LORD answer you when you are in distress; may the name of the God of Jacob protect you. May he send you *help*. (Ps. 20:1–2, emphasis added)

> We wait in hope for the Lord; he is our *help* and our shield. (Ps. 33:20, emphasis added)
>
> O house of Israel, trust in the Lord—he is their *help* and shield.
>
> O house of Aaron, trust in the Lord—he is their *help* and shield.
>
> You who fear him, trust in the Lord—he is their *help* and shield. (Ps. 115:9–11, emphasis added)

Most of the contexts are life and death, by the way, and God is your only hope. Your ezer. If he is not there beside you . . . you are dead. A better translation therefore of ezer would be "lifesaver." *Kenegdo* means alongside, or opposite to, a counterpart.

That longing in the heart of a woman to share life together as a great adventure—that comes straight from the heart of God, who also longs for this. He does not want to be an option in our lives. He does not want to be an appendage, a tagalong. Neither does any woman. God is essential. He wants us to need him—desperately. Eve is essential. She has an irreplaceable role to play. And so you'll see that women are endowed with fierce devotion, an ability to suffer great hardships, a vision to make the world a better place.

- Have you realized that God gave the Human Mission in Genesis 1:26-28 to both Adam and Eve? What part of that mission most excites you—and why?

- Describe what "ezer kenegdo" means in your own words? What does this term stir in you?

The longing in your heart to share life together as a great adventure comes from God. What current adventure would you love to step into? What do you feel is holding you back from beginning it? Spend some time talking or journaling about this with Jesus in prayer.

DAY 3
THE FALL OF EVE

When the world was young and we were innocent—both man and woman—we were naked and unashamed (Gen. 2:25). Nothing to hide. Simply . . . glorious. And while that world was young, and we, too, were young and beautiful and full of life, a corner was turned. Something happened, which we have heard about, but never fully understood, or we would see it playing itself out every day of our lives, and, more important, we would *also* see the chances given to us every day to reverse what happened.

Now the serpent was the shrewdest of all the creatures the Lord God had made. "Really?" he asked the woman. "Did God really say you must not eat any of the fruit in the garden?"

"Of course we may eat it," the woman told him. "It's only the fruit from the tree at the center of the garden that we are not allowed to eat. God says we must not eat it or even touch it, or we will die."

"You won't die!" the serpent hissed. "God knows that your eyes will be opened when you eat it. You will become just like God, knowing everything, both good and evil."

The woman was convinced. The fruit looked so fresh and delicious, and it would make her so wise! So she ate some of the fruit. She also gave some to her husband, who was with her. Then he ate it, too. (Gen. 3:1–6 NLT)

Alas.

There are no words.

Wail; beat your chest; fall to your knees; let out a long, lonesome howl of bitter remorse.

The woman was convinced. That's it? Just like that? In a matter of moments? Convinced of what? Look in your own heart—you'll see. Convinced that God was holding out on her. Convinced that she could not trust his heart toward her. Convinced that in order to have the best possible life, she must take matters into her own hands. And so she did. She is the first to fall. In disobeying God she also violated her very essence. Eve is supposed to be Adam's ezer kenegdo, like one who comes to *save*. She is to bring him life, invite him to life. Instead, she invited him to his death.

Now, to be fair, Adam doesn't exactly ride to her rescue.

> Let me ask you a question: Where is Adam, while the serpent is tempting Eve? He's standing right there: "She also gave some to her husband, who was with her, and he ate it" (3:6). The Hebrew for "with her" means right there, elbow to elbow. Adam isn't away in another part of the forest; he has no alibi. He is standing right

> there, watching the whole thing unravel. What does he do? Nothing. Absolutely nothing. He says not a word, doesn't lift a finger. [I'm indebted to Crabb, Hudson, and Andrews for pointing this out in The Silence of Adam.] He won't risk, he won't fight, and he won't rescue Eve. Our first father—the first real man—gave in to paralysis. He denied his very nature and went passive. And every man after him, every son of Adam, carries in his heart now the same failure. Every man repeats the sin of Adam, every day. We won't risk, we won't fight, and we won't rescue Eve. We truly are a chip off the old block. (*Wild at Heart*)

You can see this play itself out every day. Men, just when we need them to come through for us . . . check out. They disappear, go silent and passive. "He won't talk to me," is many a woman's lament. They won't fight for us.

- What do you think Eve was believing about God when she chose the fruit?

- Were you aware Adam was standing right by Eve when she was tempted? How does his failure to respond or fight for Eve make you feel?

- Write Genesis 3:10 here.

- Are there times when you feel afraid of being exposed? What are you afraid of? Invite Jesus in to this very place to reveal his love for you.

DAY 4 DOMINATING OR DESOLATE?

Fallen Eve tends to be grasping, reaching, controlling. We are often enchanted, like Eve, so easily falling prey to the lies of our Enemy. Having forfeited our confidence in God, we believe that in order to have the life we want, we must take matters into our own hands. And we ache with an emptiness nothing seems able to fill.

A dominating woman needs no one. She is in charge —"on top of things constantly." She is a woman who knows how to get what she wants. (Some of us might even admire that!) But consider this—there is nothing merciful about her, nothing tender, and certainly nothing vulnerable. She has forsaken essential aspects of her femininity.

Fallen Eve controls her relationships. She *refuses* to be vulnerable. And if she cannot secure her relationships, then she kills her heart's longing for intimacy so that she will be safe and in control. She becomes a woman "who doesn't need anyone—especially a man." How this plays out over the course of her life and how the wounds of her childhood shape her heart's convictions are often a complex story, one worth knowing. But beneath it all, behind it all, is a simple truth: women dominate and control because they fear their vulnerability. Far from God and far from Eden, it seems a perfectly reasonable way to live. But consider also this: "Whatever is not from faith is sin" (Rom. 14:23 NKJV). That self-protective way of relating to others has nothing to do with real loving, and nothing to do with deeply trusting God. It is our gut-level response to a dangerous world.

Controlling women are those of us who don't trust anyone else to drive our cars. Or help in our kitchens. Or speak at our retreats or our meetings. Or carry something for us. Make a decision that is "ours" to make. Suggest a different dress, agenda, restaurant, route. We room alone when we travel. We plan perfect birthday parties for our children. It might look as though we're simply "trying to be a good mom" or a good friend, but what we often do is arrange other people's lives.

Controlling women tend to be very well rewarded in this fallen world of ours. We are the ones to receive corporate promotions. We are the ones put in charge of our women's ministries. Can-Do, Bottom-Line, Get-It-Done kinds of women. Women who have never even considered that our Martha Stewart perfectionism might not be a virtue. We have never considered that by living a controlling and domineering life, we are really refusing to trust our God. And it has also never dawned on us that something precious in us is squelched, diminished, and refused. Something that God has given us to bring to the world.

If on the one side of the spectrum we find that Fallen Eve becomes hard, rigid, and controlling, then on the other side we find women who are desolate, needy, far too vulnerable.

Desolate women are ruled by the aching abyss within them. These are the women who buy books like *Men Who Hate Women and the Women Who Love Them* and *Women Who Love Too Much* and *Co-dependent No More*. They are consumed by a hunger for relationship. A friend of ours, a young man in his twenties, was lamenting how much his mom calls him. "How often does she call?" I asked, thinking he might be exaggerating. "Every day." Whoa. Every day is too often for a mother to call her adult son who has left home.

Hiding women are those of us who never speak up at a Bible study or PTA council or any kind of meeting. Who, when we pass a beautiful dress in a window, say to ourselves, "I could never wear that." We stay busy at family gatherings and parties we can't avoid. We'd rather go to a movie than out to dinner with a friend. We don't initiate sex with our husbands ever. We dismiss every compliment. We relinquish major decisions to others.

Like Eve after she tasted the forbidden fruit, we women hide. We hide behind our makeup. We hide behind our humor. We hide with angry silences and punishing withdrawals. We hide our truest selves and offer only what we believe is wanted, what is safe. We act in self-protective ways and refuse to offer what we truly see, believe, and know. We will not risk rejection or looking like a fool. We have spoken in the past and been met with blank stares and mocking guffaws. We will not do it again. We hide because we are afraid. We have been wounded and wounded deeply. People have sinned against us and we have sinned as well. To hide means to remain safe, to hurt less. At least that is what we think. And so by hiding, we take matters into our own hands. We don't return to our God with our broken and desperate hearts. And it has never occurred to us that in all our hiding, something precious in us is also squelched, diminished, and refused—something God needs so very, very much for us to bring to the world.

- On the spectrum for Fallen Eve, do you tend to land more on the Controlling or Desolate side? What's an example of how this plays out in your life and relationships?

- Looking back, was your mother more controlling or desolate? How do you think this may have affected you growing up?

- Whether we're more domineering or desolate, what we've actually been doing is hiding. Do you know what has caused you to hide in your life? Invite Jesus in to tend that very place, then prayerfully ask God what the affect of that has been on your life with Jesus, on your own life and on your relationships.

INDULGING

Whether we tend to dominate and control, or withdraw in our desolation and hide, still . . . the ache remains. The deep longings in our hearts as women just won't go away. And so we indulge.

We buy ourselves something nice when we aren't feeling appreciated. We "allow" ourselves a second helping of ice cream or a super-sized something when we are lonely and our hearts need soothing. We move into a fantasy world to find some water for our thirsty hearts. Romance novels (a billion-dollar industry), soap operas, talk shows, gossip, the myriads of women's magazines all feed an inner life of relational dreaming and voyeurism that substitutes—for a while—for the real thing. But none of these really satisfy, and so we find ourselves trying to fill the remaining emptiness with our little indulgences (we call them "bad habits"). Brent Curtis calls them our "little affairs of the heart." God calls them "broken cisterns" (Jer. 2:13). They are what we give our hearts away to instead of giving them to the heart of God.

We daydream our way through traffic. We imagine meaningful conversations or difficult ones where we speak brilliantly. We spend our imaginations on cheap novels, picturing ourselves as the heroine—winsome, pursued, beautiful. We are endlessly creative in our indulgent pursuits, our adulteries of the heart. Certainly, we do not limit ourselves to just one.

Take a moment and consider yours. Where do you go instead of to God when the ache of your heart begins to make itself known? Spending too much money, gambling, bingeing, purging, shopping, drinking, working, cleaning, exercising, too many movies, sitcoms, talk shows, even our negative emotions can become indulgences. When we camp our hearts in self-doubt, condemning thoughts, or even shame because those emotions have become familiar and comfortable, we are faithlessly indulging rather than allowing our deep ache to draw us to God.

Unfortunately, our indulgences make us feel better . . . for a while. They seem to "work," but really only increase our need to indulge again. This is the nightmare of addiction. But it goes far beyond "drugs." We give our hearts to all sorts of other "lovers" that demand our attention, demand we indulge again. When we taste something that we think is good, our longings cease to ache, for a minute, but later we find ourselves empty once more, needing to be filled again and again.

The ways we find to numb our aches, our longings, and our pain are not benign. They are malignant. They entangle themselves in our souls like a cancer and, once attached, become addictions that are both cruel and relentless. Though we seek them out for a little relief from the sorrows of life, addictions turn on us and imprison us in chains that separate us from the heart of God and others as well. It is a lonely prison of our own making, each chain forged in the fire of our indulgent choice. Yet, "Our lovers have so intertwined themselves with our identity that to give them up feels like personal death . . . We wonder if it is possible to live without them" (The Sacred Romance). Yes, we are, each of us, to greater and lesser degrees, still in bondage. But the good news is that "God has not deserted us in our bondage" (Ezra 9:9).

We need not be ashamed that our hearts ache; that we need and thirst and hunger for much more. All of our hearts ache. All of our hearts are at some level unsatisfied and longing. It is our insatiable need for more that drives us to our God. What we need to see is that all our controlling and our hiding, all our indulging, actually serves to separate us from our hearts. We lose touch with those longings that make us women. And the substitutes never, ever resolve the deeper issue of our souls.

- What is the primary ache of your heart? Try to put into words what you most long for.

- Other than God, where do you tend to go when the ache of your heart makes itself known?

- In the moment, what do you hope that particular indulgence will do for you? Has it delivered what you've wanted . . . or had another, less desirable impact? Spend some time in prayer and ask Jesus to help you turn to Him the next time you want to reach for something other than him to meet your heart's true need.

CLOSING THOUGHTS

Sometimes it can be difficult to consider the ways that we act out of a fallen place. It can be painful and usher in shame. That is not what God wants. Certainly, we want to repent of the ways we are living out of fear and not out of faith. But the invitation from God to take a deeper look at the ways that we hide are really an invitation to deeper intimacy with him with the goal of knowing him better and increasing in wholeheartedness. It is worth it. We can take a deeper look because God loves us and there is mercy in his eyes.

SESSION THREE

THE WOUND AND THE HEALER

GROUP STUDY

"These words are razors to my wounded heart."
—**William Shakespeare**

Welcome!

Welcome to Session Three of *Captivating*. If something stood out to you in your personal study, share briefly with your group.

Let's dive in!

Core Scripture

Look up Psalm 56:8 and write it in the space below.

Invite several women to read various translations of the passage aloud. Listen for fresh insights and share any thoughts about this verse with the group.

VIDEO

Watch the video segment for Session Three, streaming or on DVD. This summary is provided for your benefit as well as space to take additional notes.

Summary

It's true that some women's lives look perfect to us from a distance. But only from a distance. If we get close, we will learn the truth.

Your joys matter and your sorrows matter. So do your wounds.

We don't revisit the wounds of our lives simply to feel sorry for ourselves, but for the purposes of God to heal us. In order to obtain that, we have to be honest.

God invites us to grieve our wounds and to receive his comfort and then his healing. But to be healed, we must once again let God tenderly open our wounds and expose them to his light, to his love, and to his truth.

When Jesus first entered the synagogue to begin his earthly mission, he opened the Holy Scriptures and read from the book of Isaiah. When he finished, he proclaimed that in that moment, the Scripture had been fulfilled. Jesus read Isaiah 61.

The offer from our God is to heal our broken hearts and to set free the places that are held captive within us. All of us have broken hearts. All of us are held captive in varying degrees. In order to receive the healing that God has for us, we must bring him our wounded hearts.

NOTES

GROUP DISCUSSION

Choose the questions that work best for your group.

1. In what way did Juanita's story reveal how we as women can be wounded?

2. What was evoked for you during this session?

3. How were these core questions answered when you were a little girl? Pick one to share with the group:

   - Do you delight in me?

   - Do you see me?

   - Am I captivating?

4. No one has a pain free life. We all live in a fallen world. What were the messages you received as a girl through your wounds?

5. Who is Jesus coming for when he quotes Isaiah 61—and what is he offering?

6. How are the two things Jesus offers in Isaiah 61 relevant to you?

7. Can you share with the group a place in your heart or in your life that you would like Jesus to come for you—and why that place needs healing?

Closing Prayer

Leader or volunteer, close your group time in prayer:

> *My dear Jesus,*
> *Thank you for coming to rescue me—to heal me and to free me from every captive place. Lord, I know that part of my healing will come as I forgive those that hurt me. You have forgiven me all my sins at the cross. Please help me to forgive others as well. It's hard, Lord. Would you help me? Jesus, by your grace, with your strength and in your Name, I forgive ________ ______ for ________________. I release them to you. I lay them down at your feet. I bring your cross and your blood between us. Please cleanse me of my sin again, and cleanse me of theirs. Forever. I ask you to come for me in every wounded place and bring me your healing. Do for me Jesus all that you came to do. In Jesus' Name, I pray. Amen.*

Recommended Reading

Before your group gathers for the next session, read Chapter 5 (*A Special Hatred)* in the book *Captivating*. Use the space provided to write any key points or questions you want to bring to the next group meeting.

BETWEEN-SESSIONS PERSONAL STUDY

In this section, you're invited to further explore the material we've covered this week from *Captivating*. Each day offers a short reading from Chapter 4 (*Wounded*) or Chapter 6 (*Healing the Wound*) of John and Stasi's book—along with reflection questions designed to take you deeper into the themes of this week's study.

Journal or just jot a few thoughts after each question. At the start of the next session, there will be a few minutes to share any insights . . . but the primary goal of these questions is for your personal growth and private reflection.

HOW OUR WOUNDS SHAPE US

The wounds that we received as young girls did not come alone. They brought messages with them, messages that struck at the core of our hearts, right in the place of our Question. Our wounds strike at the core of our femininity. The damage done to our feminine hearts through the wounds we received is made much worse by the horrible things we believe about ourselves as a result. As children, we didn't have the faculties to process and sort through what was happening to us. Our parents were godlike. We believed them to be right. If we were overwhelmed or belittled or hurt or abused, we believed that somehow it was because of *us*—the problem was with *us*.

As a result of the wounds we receive growing up, we come to believe that some part of us, maybe every part of us, is marred. Shame enters in and makes its crippling home deep within our hearts. Shame is what makes us look away, so we avoid eye contact with strangers and friends. Shame is that feeling that haunts us, the sense that if someone really knew us, they would shake their heads in disgust and run away. Shame makes us feel, no, *believe*, that we do not measure up—not to the world's standards, the church's standards, or our own standards.

Shame causes us to hide. We are afraid of being truly seen, and so we hide our truest selves and offer only what we believe is wanted. If we are a dominating kind of woman, we offer our "expertise." If we are a desolate kind of woman, we offer our "service." We are silent and do not say what we see or know when it is different from what others are saying, because we think we must be wrong. We refuse to bring the weight of our lives, who God has made us to be, to bear on others out of a fear of being rejected.

Shame makes us feel very uncomfortable with our beauty. Women are beautiful, every single one of us. It is one of the glorious ways that we bear the image of God. But few of us believe we are beautiful, and fewer still are comfortable with it. We either think we don't have any beauty or if we do, that it's dangerous and bad. So we hide our beauty physically or we neutralize our beauty by putting up protective, defensive walls that warn others to keep their distance.

Over the years we've come to see that the only thing more tragic than the things that have happened to us is what we have done with them.

Words were said, painful words. Things were done, awful things. And they shaped us. Something inside of us *shifted*. We embraced the messages of our wounds. We accepted a twisted view of ourselves. And from that we chose a way of relating to our world. We made a vow never to be in that place again. We adopted strategies to protect ourselves from being hurt again. A woman who is living out of a broken, wounded heart is a woman who is living a self-protective life. She may not be aware of it, but it is true. It's our way of trying to "save ourselves."

We also developed ways of trying to get something of the love our hearts cried out for. The ache is there. Despite the best face we put on our lives, the ache is there. As Proverbs says, "Even in laughter the heart may ache" (14:13). Our desperate need for love and affirmation, our thirst for some taste of romance and adventure and beauty is there. So we turned to boys or to food or to a myriad of available distractions;

we lost ourselves in our work or at church or in some sort of service. All this adds up to the women we are today. Much of what we call our "personalities" is actually the mosaic of our choices for self-protection plus our plan to get something of the love we were created for.

The problem is our plan has nothing to do with God.

- It's often easier to identify our wounds more than the messages that came with them. In the space below, write one or more wounds you experienced growing up—and the message that each brought with it.

- How has shame played a role in your life?

- Write Proverbs 14:13 below. In what ways has this ache of the heart caused you to seek relief or validation outside of God?

DAY 2 THE OFFER

The purposes of Jesus Christ are not finished when one of his precious ones is forgiven. Not at all. Would a good father feel satisfied when his daughter is rescued from a car accident, but left in ICU? Doesn't he want her to be healed as well? So God has much more in mind for us. Listen to this passage from Isaiah (it might help to read it very slowly, carefully, out loud to yourself) . . .

> The Spirit of the Sovereign Lord is on me,
> because the Lord has anointed me
> to preach good news to the poor.
> He has sent me to bind up the brokenhearted,
> to proclaim freedom for the captives
> and release from darkness for the prisoners,
> to proclaim the year of the Lord's favor
> and the day of vengeance of our God,
> to comfort all who mourn,
> and provide for those who grieve in Zion—
> to bestow on them a crown of beauty instead of ashes,
> the oil of gladness
> instead of mourning,
> and a garment of praise
> instead of a spirit of despair. (Is. 61:1–3)

This is the passage that Jesus pointed to when he began his ministry here on earth. Of all the Scriptures he could have chosen, this is the one he picked on the day he first publicly announced his mission. It must be important to him. It must be central. What does it mean? It's supposed to be really good news, that's clear. It has something to do with healing hearts, setting someone free. Let me try and state it in words more familiar to us.

> God has sent me on a mission.
> I have some great news for you.
> God has sent me to restore and release something.
> And that something is you.
> I am here to give you back your heart and set you free.
> I am furious at the Enemy who did this to you, and I will fight against him.
> Let me comfort you.
> For, dear one, I will bestow beauty upon you
> where you have known only devastation.
> Joy, in the places of your deep sorrow.
> And I will robe your heart in thankful praise
> in exchange for your resignation and despair.

Now that is an offer worth considering. What if it were true? I mean, what if Jesus really *could* and *would* do this for your broken heart, your wounded feminine soul? Read it again, and ask him, *Jesus—is this true for me? Would you do this for me?*

He can, and he will . . . if you'll let him.

You are the glorious Image Bearer of the Lord Jesus Christ—the crown of his creation. You have been assaulted. You have fallen to your own resources. Your Enemy has seized upon your wounds and your sins to pin your heart down. Now the Son of God has come to ransom you, and to heal your broken, wounded, bleeding heart, and to set you free from bondage. He came for the brokenhearted captives. That's me. That's you. He came to restore the glorious creation that you are. And then set you free . . . to be yourself.

> The LORD their God will save them on that day
> as the flock of his people.
> They will sparkle in his land
> like jewels in a crown.
> How attractive and beautiful they will be! (Zech. 9:16–17)

Here is the core reason we wrote this book: to let you know that the healing of your feminine heart is available, and to help you find that healing. To help you find the restoration which we all long for and which is central to Jesus' mission. Let him take you by the hand now and walk with you through your restoration and release.

- What does the thought that God doesn't just want to forgive us but desires to heal us do for your heart?

- What most stands out to you from the passage of Isaiah 61:1-3? Why?

- What is the reason given for why John and Stasi wrote this book? Are you willing to trust this is possible and enter into this journey? Take the leap and ask God to do it for you.

BEGINNING THE HEALING JOURNEY

To enter the journey toward the healing of your feminine heart, all it requires is a, Yes. Okay. A simple turning in the heart. Like the Prodigal we wake one day to see that the life we've constructed is no life at all. We let desire speak to us again; we let our hearts have a voice, and what the voice usually says is, *This isn't working. My life is a disaster. Jesus—I'm sorry. Forgive me. Please come for me.* So begin here, pray just this:

> *Jesus, I give myself to you. I give my life to you. I surrender me—totally and completely. Forgive all my sins, my hurtful ways. Forgive all my self-protecting and all of my chasing after other comforters. Come for me now, dear Lord. Come and be my Savior, my Healer, my Love.*

There is a famous passage of Scripture that many people have heard in the context of an invitation to know Christ as Savior. "Behold, I stand at the door and knock. If anyone hears My voice and opens the door, I will come in" (Rev 3:20 NKJV). He does not force himself upon us. He knocks, and waits for us to ask him in. There is an initial step, the first step of this, which we call salvation. We hear Christ knocking and we open our hearts to him as Savior. It is the first turning. But the principle of this "knocking and waiting for permission to come in" remains true well into our Christian life.

Give him permission. Give him access to your broken heart. Ask him to come to *these* places.

> *Yes, Jesus, yes. I do invite you in. Come to my heart in these shattered places. [You know what they are—ask him there. Is it the abuse? The loss of your father? The jealousy of your mother? Ask him in.] Come to me, my Savior. I open this door of my heart. I give you permission to heal my wounds. Come to me here. Come for me here.*

Your wounds brought messages with them. Lots of messages. Somehow they all usually land in the same place. They had a similar theme. "You're worthless." "You're not a woman." "You're too much . . . and not enough." "You're a disappointment." "You are repulsive." On and on they go. Because they were delivered with such pain, they *felt* true. They pierced our hearts, and they seemed so true. So we accepted the messages as fact. We embraced them as the verdict on us.

As we said earlier, the vows we made as children act like a deep-seated agreement with the messages of our wounds. "Fine. If that's how it is, then that's how it is. I'll live my life in the following way . . ." The vows we made acted like a kind of covenant with the messages that came with our deep wounds. Those childhood vows are very dangerous things. We must renounce them. *Before* we are entirely convinced that they aren't true, we must reject the messages of our wounds. It's a way of unlocking the door to Jesus. Agreements lock the door from the inside. Renouncing the agreements unlocks the door to him.

> *Jesus, forgive me for embracing these lies. This is not what you have said of me. You said I am your daughter, your beloved, your cherished one. I renounce the agreements I made with [name the specific messages you've been living with. "I'm stupid. I'm ugly." You know what they are.] I*

renounce the agreements I've been making with these messages all these years. Bring the truth here, oh Spirit of Truth. I reject these lies.

- What is described as the first step of the healing journey? Describe if this beginning point seems simple or hard to you—and why.

- How does the passage in Revelation 3:20 relate to giving Jesus access to your heart? And what is your role in the process?

- What agreements do you need to renounce or what lies do you need to reject? Write them down in the space below. Then cross them out as you actively pray to God and reject/reounce them.

DAY 4

FORGIVENESS AND HEALING

Okay—now for a hard step (as if the others have been easy). A real step of courage and will. We must forgive those who hurt us. The reason is simple: Bitterness and unforgiveness set their hooks deep in our hearts; they are chains that hold us captive to the wounds and the messages of those wounds. Until you forgive, you remain their prisoner. Paul warns us that unforgiveness and bitterness can wreck our lives and the lives of others (Eph. 4:31; Heb. 12:15). We have to let it all go.

> Forgive as the Lord forgave you. (Col. 3:13)

Now—listen carefully. Forgiveness is a *choice*. It is not a feeling—don't try and feel forgiving. It is an act of the will. "Don't wait to forgive until you feel like forgiving," wrote Neil Anderson. "You will never get there. Feelings take time to heal after the choice to forgive is made." We allow God to bring the hurt up from our past, for "if your forgiveness doesn't visit the emotional core of your life, it will be incomplete," said Anderson. We acknowledge that it hurt, that it mattered, and we choose to extend forgiveness to our fathers, our mothers, those who hurt us. This is *not* saying, "It didn't really matter"; it is not saying, "I probably deserved part of it anyway." Forgiveness says, "It was wrong. Very wrong. It mattered, hurt me deeply. And I release you. I give you to God. I will not be your captive here any longer."

It might help to remember that those who hurt you were also deeply wounded themselves. They were broken hearts, broken when they were young, and they fell captive to the Enemy. They were in fact pawns in his hands. This doesn't absolve them of the choices they made, the things they did. It just helps us to let them go—to realize that they were shattered souls themselves, used by our true Enemy in his war against femininity.

Now, ask Jesus to heal you. We turn from our self-redemptive strategies. We open the door of our hurting heart to Jesus. We renounce the agreements we made with the messages of our wounds, renounce any vows we made. We forgive those who harmed us. And then, with an open heart, we simply ask Jesus to heal us.

> *Jesus, come to me and heal my heart. Come to the shattered places within me. Come for the little girl that was wounded. Come and hold me in your arms, and heal me. Do for me what you promised to do—heal my broken heart and set me free.*

- Write Colossians 3:13 below. Why is this such a simple verse to understand but such a hard concept to actually do?

- Have you considered before that forgiveness is a choice rather than a feeling? Who do you need to choose to forgive?

- To turn from your self-redemptive strategies can seem overhwhelming. But remember, it isn't all up to you. What is currently standing in the way of believing that God can heal your heart and set you free? Can you release that to God—trusting him for the outcome?

DAY 5 GOD AS PROTECTOR AND FATHER

In the beautiful passage of Isaiah 61, God promises "freedom for the captives and release from darkness for the prisoners" (v. 1). He goes on to proclaim "vengeance" against our enemies (v. 2). Our wounds, our vows, and the agreements we've made with the messages all give ground to the Enemy in our lives. Paul warns about this in Ephesians 4 when he says—writing to Christians—"and do not give the devil a foothold" (v. 27). There are things you've struggled with all your life—self-doubt, anger, depression, shame, addiction, fear. You probably thought that those were your fault too.

But they are not. They came from the Enemy who wanted to take your heart captive, make you a prisoner of darkness. To be sure, we complied. We allowed those strongholds to form when we mishandled our wounds and made those vows. But Jesus has forgiven us for all of that, and now he wants to set us free.

Ask him to destroy your enemies. He promised to, after all. Ask Jesus to release your heart from captivity to these things.

> *Jesus, come and rescue me. Set me free from [you know what you need freedom from—name it]. Release me from darkness. Bring your vengeance on my enemies. I reject them and ask you to take them to judgment. Set my heart free.*

God is our protector against the Enemy. And he is also our good Father.

Every little girl was made to live in a world with a father who loves her unconditionally. She first learns who God is, what he is like, and how he feels about her from her earthly dad. God is "Our Father, who art in heaven." He means initially to reveal himself to his daughters and his sons through the love of our dads. We were meant to know a father's love, be kept safe in it, be protected by it, and blossom there.

There is a core part of our hearts that was made for Daddy. Made for his strong and tender love. That part is still there, and longing. Open it to Jesus and to your Father God. Ask him to come and love you there. Meet you there. We've all tried so hard to find the fulfillment of this love in other people, and it never, ever works. Let us give this treasure back to the One who can love us best.

> *Father, I need your love. Come to the core of my heart. Come and bring your love for me. Help me to know you for who you really are—not as I see my earthly father. Reveal yourself to me. Reveal your love for me. Tell me what I mean to you. Come, and father me.*

- Would it help your healing journey to get to know God more as both your protector and Father? Which way seems the most unfamiliar to you at this time–and why?

- Have you assumed that all you've struggled with your whole life has been your fault? How does it change things to realize it came from the Enemy?

- Has your earthly father been a helpful or unhelpful role model in knowing God as Father? Ask God to help you know him ever more deeply as he truly is.

CLOSING THOUGHTS

Friends, this is a critically important session. Please spend some time revisiting the prayers here and in the book and slowly pray them for yourself. The healing of your heart and your restoration as a woman are central to the purposes of Jesus. You are worth the time. You are worth the effort. In fact, God has proven that you are worth everything. You are worth the precious blood.

SESSION FOUR

A SPECIAL HATRED

GROUP STUDY

"All who hate me whisper about me, imagining the worst."
—Psalm 41:7 NLT

Welcome!

Welcome to Session Four of *Captivating*. If something stood out to you in your personal study, share briefly with your group.

Let's dive in!

Core Scripture

Look up 1 Peter 5:8–9 and write it in the space below.

Invite several women to read various translations of the passage aloud. Listen for fresh insights and share any thoughts about this verse with the group.

VIDEO

Watch the video segment for Session Four, streaming or on DVD. This summary is provided for your benefit as well as space to take additional notes.

Summary

If you will listen carefully to any woman's story, you will hear a theme: the assault on her heart. It might be obvious, or it might be more subtle.. Either way, the wounds continue to come long after we've "grown up," but they all seem to speak the same message.

What is to account for the systemic, often brutal, nearly universal assault on femininity? Where does this come from?

You have an enemy.

Spiritual warfare is no strange thing. Peter assumes that every Christian is under regular, spiritual assault (1 Peter 5:8–9). It is a normal part of the Christian life. It's true. And it's true for you.

In John 10:10, Jesus tells us: The thief comes only to steal and kill and destroy; I have come that they may have life, and have it to the full.

Too often, in church, we only hear about the second part of this verse. But Jesus said them in the same breath. In order to have the life that Jesus wants us to have, we have to be aware that we have an enemy who is busy trying to steal, kill, and destroy our lives and the lives of those we know and love.

You are under regular, spiritual assault. When you believe that the devil has no fiery darts flying your way, then you believe that every wicked, hurtful thing that comes your way is either your fault or God's. It destroys your relationship with him. And the devil just loves that.

In order to have the life God wants for you, you must rise up and take your stand in him. There is a fierceness that God placed in women and this is what it is for. Men aren't our enemy. Women aren't the enemy. But you have one. There is no reason to fear him, but you must not close your eyes, plug your ears and hope he just goes away. He won't. You must resist.

NOTES

GROUP DISCUSSION

Choose the questions that work best for your group.

1. The enemy comes against each of us in unique ways. How did you see this at play in Sue's story?

2. What was evoked for you during this session?

3. Stasi reveals that regular spiritual assault is a normal part of the Christian life. How might accepting this fact change how you approach each day?

4. What was your perception of spiritual warfare before this session?

5. Is your understanding of spiritual warfare now different? How so?

6. When we don't believe there's an enemy, we tend to think every hurtful thing coming our way is either our fault or God's. Describe how you've experienced this—and what the effect was on your heart or relationship with God.

7. In the video, Sue confesses she struggles with comparison. How do you tend to compare yourself to others—and what is the usual result of doing so?

8. What does James 4:7 say happens when we submit to God and resist the enemy? Have you found this effective tool in overcoming the Enemy?

Closing Prayer

Leader or volunteer, close your group time in prayer:

> *My dear Jesus,*
> *Thank you for opening my eyes to the spiritual reality that is around me. Too often, I forget that I was born into a world at war. Strengthen me, Lord to submit to you and to resist the devil. I choose to obey your Word and make my thoughts captive to the obedience of Christ and believe the Truth and only the Truth—even about myself. I fix my gaze on you, Jesus, and I ask You to heal the places in me that have been wounded by the assault of the enemy. Train me Jesus to stand firm, to rise up and to bring your Kingdom. In Jesus' Name. Amen.*

Recommended Reading

Before your group gathers for the next session, read Chapter 8 (*A Beauty to Unveil)* in the book *Captivating*. Use the space provided to write any key points or questions you want to bring to the next group meeting.

BETWEEN-SESSIONS PERSONAL STUDY

In this section, you're invited to further explore the material we've covered this week from *Captivating.* Each day offers a short reading from Chapter 5 (*A Special Hatred*) of John and Stasi's book—along with reflection questions designed to take you deeper into the themes of this week's study.

Journal or just jot a few thoughts after each question. At the start of the next session, there will be a few minutes to share any insights . . . but the primary goal of these questions is for your personal growth and private reflection.

DAY 1

WHAT IS REALLY GOING ON HERE?

The story of the treatment of women down through the ages is not a noble history. It has noble moments in it, to be sure, but taken as a whole, women have endured what seems to be a special hatred ever since we left Eden. The story we just cited is but one of thousands coming not just out of the Sudan but from many war-torn countries like it. UN Peacekeeping troops say that in 2009 alone, in the war raging in the Congo, more than 7,500 rapes were reported.[1] They know the actual number is much higher. Sexual assault is a far too common and effective weapon in these "civil" wars. Honestly, what do you make of the degradation, the abuse, and the open assault that women around the world have endured—are enduring even now?

Up until about seventy years ago, little girls born in China who were not left by the side of the road to die (boys are the preferred child) often had their feet bound to keep them small. Small feet were a sign of feminine beauty and were prized by would-be husbands. They were also crippling, which is quite possibly another reason why men thought them a good thing. Women who had their feet bound as children hobbled in pain throughout their lives, unable to walk freely or quickly. Although the practice was outlawed in the 1930s, it continued long after.

You might know that through the thousands of years of Jewish history recorded in the Old Testament, Jewish women were considered property with no legal rights (as they were and are in many cultures). They were not allowed to study the Law, nor to formally educate their children. They had a segregated place in the synagogue. It was common practice for a Jewish man to add to his morning prayers, "Thank you, God, for not making me a Gentile, a woman, or a slave."

A Chinese proverb says that "a woman should be like water; she should take no form and have no voice." An Indian proverb says, "Educating a woman is like watering your neighbor's garden," meaning, of course, that educating a woman is both foolish and a waste of time. In Hinduism, a woman has less value than a cow. We are not talking ancient history here. We are talking about today. Now. In Islam, a woman requires three men to verify her story in court in order for her testimony to be valid. Her testimony, her worth, is one third of a man's.

The story goes well beyond the denial of education and legal rights. Clitoridectomy is the removal, or circumcision, of the clitoris. A painful, horrible practice, female genital mutilation continues today and is performed on girls when they reach about five years old. Done primarily in Africa, the surgery is often performed in the wilderness with the use of a sharp rock. Infections are common. Sometimes the girl dies. A woman is forever maimed, never able to enjoy sexual pleasure—and that is the point. A sexually aware woman is thought to be dangerous. Femininity must be controlled.

Sexual violence against women is rampant throughout the world. It is also rampant against little girls. More than one million girls are sold into the sex trade every year. Dear God—what is to account for the systemic, often brutal, nearly universal assault on women? Where does this come from? Do not make the mistake of believing that "men are the enemy." Certainly men have had a hand in this, and will have a day of reckoning before their Maker. But you will not understand this story—or your story—until you begin to see the actual Forces behind this and get a grip on their motives.

Where does this hatred for women, seen all over the world, come from? Why is it so diabolical?

- What is most shocking to you about the systemic, often brutal, nearly universal assault on femininity in world history?

- How have you personally experienced this hatred or assault in your life?

- While men certainly have and do play a role in the abuse of women, how would you describe the greater Forces behind this rampant evil?

DAY 2
A SPECIAL HATRED

The assault on femininity—its long history, its utter viciousness—cannot be understood apart from the spiritual forces of evil we are warned against in the Scriptures. This is not to say that men (and women, for they, too, assault women) have no accountability in their treatment of women. Not at all. It is simply to say that no explanation for the assault upon Eve and her daughters is sufficient unless it opens our eyes to the Prince of Darkness and his special hatred of femininity.

Turn your attention again to the events that took place in the garden of Eden. Notice—who does the Evil One go after? Who does Satan single out for his move against the human race? He could have chosen Adam . . . but he didn't. Satan went after Eve. He set his sights on her. Have you ever wondered why? It might have been that he, like any predator, chose what he believed to be the weaker of the two. But we believe there are other reasons. Why does Satan make Eve the focus of his assault on humanity?

You may know that Satan was first named Lucifer, or Son of the Morning. It infers a glory, a brightness or radiance unique to him. In the days of his former glory he was appointed a guardian angel. Many believe he was the captain of the angel armies of God. The guardian of the glory of the Lord.

> You were the seal of perfection,
> full of wisdom and perfect in beauty.
> You were in Eden,
> the garden of God;
> every precious stone adorned you:
> ruby, topaz and emerald,
> chrysolite, onyx and jasper,
> sapphire, turquoise and beryl.
> Your settings and mountings were made of gold;
> on the day you were created they were prepared.
> You were anointed as a guardian cherub,
> for so I ordained you.
> You were on the holy mount of God;
> you walked among the fiery stones. (Ezek. 28:12–14)

Perfect in beauty. That is the key. Lucifer was gorgeous. He was breathtaking. And it was his ruin. Pride entered Lucifer's heart. The angel came to believe he was being cheated somehow. He craved the worship that was being given to God for himself. He didn't merely want to play a noble role in the Story; he wanted the Story to be about him. He wanted to be the star. He wanted the attention, the adoration for himself. ("Mirror, Mirror, on the wall . . .")

> Your heart became proud
> on account of your beauty,
> and you corrupted your wisdom
> because of your splendor. (Ezek. 28:17)

Satan fell *because* of his beauty. Now his heart for revenge is to assault beauty. He destroys it in the natural world wherever he can. Strip mines, oil spills, fires, pollution, Chernobyl. He wreaks destruction on the glory of God in the earth like a psychopath committed to destroying great works of art.

But *most* especially, he hates Eve.

Because she is captivating, uniquely glorious, and he cannot be. She is the incarnation of the Beauty of God. More than anything else in all creation, she embodies the glory of God. She allures the world to God. He hates it with a jealousy we can only imagine.

And there is more. The Evil One also hates Eve because she gives life. Women give birth, not men. Women nourish life. And they also bring life into the world soulfully, relationally, spiritually—in everything they touch. Satan was a murderer from the beginning (John 8:44). He brings death. His is a kingdom of death. Ritual sacrifices, genocide, the Holocaust, abortion—those are his ideas. And thus Eve is his greatest human threat, for she brings life. She is a lifesaver and a life giver. Eve means "life" or "life producer." "Adam named his wife Eve, because she would become the mother of all the living" (Gen. 3:20).

Put those two things together—that Eve incarnates the Beauty of God *and* she gives life to the world. Satan's bitter heart cannot bear it. He assaults her with a special hatred. History removes any doubt about this. Do you begin to see it?

- Why do you think Satan made Eve the focus of his assault against humanity?

- Based on Ezekiel 28:17, what happened to the Enemy's heart and wisdom—and what was the cause of his downfall?

- In addition to her beauty, what is the second reason why the Evil One hates Eve? How do you see this hatred play out in our world today?

DAY 3

YOUR BEAUTY AND YOUR POWER

Think of the great stories—in nearly all of them, the villain goes after the Hero's true love. He turns his sights on the *Beauty*. Magua goes after Cora in *The Last of the Mohicans*. Longshanks goes after Murron in Braveheart. Commodus goes after Maximus's wife in *Gladiator*. The Witch attacks Sleeping Beauty. The stepsisters assault Cinderella. Satan goes after Eve.

This explains an awful lot. It is not meant to scare you. Actually, it will shed so much light on your life's story, if you will let it. Most of you thought the things that have happened to you were somehow *your fault*—that you deserved it. If only you had been prettier or smarter or done more or pleased them, somehow it wouldn't have happened. You would have been loved. They wouldn't have hurt you.

And most of you are living with the guilt that somehow it's your fault you aren't more deeply pursued now. That you do not have an essential role in a great adventure. That you have no beauty to unveil. The message of our wounds nearly always is, "This is because of you. This is what you deserve." It changes things to realize that, no, it is because you are glorious that these things happened. It is because you are powerful. It is because you are a major threat to the kingdom of darkness. Because you uniquely carry the glory of God to the world.

You are hated because of your beauty and power.

- Think of your favorite movies. Briefly list the titles below—and describe how the villian goes after the Hero's true love in these stories.

- Do you view yourself as God's true love? How might doing so explain your story in a way that makes more sense than blaming all that's going wrong on either you or God?

- You are a major threat to the kingdom of darkness. What is one way you can begin to embrace your beauty and power that will carry the glory of God to the world?

THE LIE THAT YOU ARE ALONE

To every woman, Satan has whispered, "You are alone," or "When they see who you really are, you will be alone," or "No one will ever truly come for you."

Take a moment. Quiet your heart and ask yourself, "Is this a message I have believed, feared, lived with?" Not only do most women fear they will ultimately be abandoned by the men in their lives—they fear it from other women as well. That they will be abandoned by their friends and left alone. It's time to reveal this pervasive threat, this crippling fear, this terrible lie.

I'm reminded of a scene from *The Two Towers*, the second film in The Lord of the Rings trilogy. It takes place in the land of Rohan, in the hall of the king, in the chambers of the lovely Éowyn. She is the king's niece, the only Lady of the court. Her dearest cousin, Théodred, the son of the king, has just died from wounds he received in battle. She is grieving her loss when Wormtongue—supposed counselor to the king but a treacherous, vile creature—slinks into her chambers and begins to weave his spell around the unprotected maiden.

Wormtongue: O . . . he must have died sometime during the night. What a tragedy for the king to lose his only son and heir. I understand his passing is hard to accept. Especially now that your brother has deserted you. [Wormtongue arranged for his banishment.]

Éowyn: Leave me alone, snake!

Wormtongue: O, but you are alone. Who knows what you have spoken to the darkness in bitter watches of the night when all your life seems to shrink, the walls of your bower closing in about you. A hushed, tremulsome, wild thing. (He takes her face in his hand.) So fair . . . and so cold. Like a morning with pale spring, still clinging to winter's chill.

Éowyn: (Finally pulling away from his clutch.) Your words are poison.[2]

"Oh, but you are alone." This is the way of the Evil One toward you. He plays upon a woman's worst fear: abandonment. He arranges for her to be abandoned, and he puts his spin on every event he can to make it seem like abandonment.

- What, in your story, makes it easy to believe the lie that you are alone and that everything is up to you?

- What most stands out to you in this scene from *Lord of the Rings* . . . and why?

- How has the fear of abandonement shaped your story?

DAY 5
THERE IS HOPE

You won't begin to understand the long and sustained assault on femininity, on women, until you see it as part of something much larger. The most wicked force the world has ever known. The Enemy bears a special hatred for Eve. If you believe he has any role in the history of this world, you cannot help but see it.

The Evil One had a hand in all that has happened to you. If he didn't arrange for the assault directly—and certainly human sin has a large enough role to play—then he made sure he drove the message of the wounds home into your heart. He is the one who has dogged your heels with shame and self-doubt and accusation. He is the one who offers the false comforters to you in order to deepen your bondage. He is the one who has done these things in order to prevent your restoration. For that is what he fears. He fears who you are; what you are; what you might become. He fears your beauty and your life-giving heart.

Now listen to the voice of your King. This is God's heart toward you:

> For Zion's sake I will not keep silent,
> for Jerusalem's sake I will not remain quiet,
> till her righteousness shines out like the dawn [until you
> shimmer],
> her salvation like a blazing torch.

The nations will see your righteousness,
and all kings your glory [your beauty];
you will be called by a new name
that the mouth of the LORD will bestow.
You will be a crown of splendor in the LORD's hand [the crown of creation],
a royal diadem in the hand of your God.
No longer will they call you Deserted,
or name your land Desolate.
But you will be called Hephzibah [my delight is in her],
and your land Beulah [married];
for the LORD will take delight in you,
and your land will be married.
As a young man marries a maiden [he pursues her, romances her] . . .
as a bridegroom rejoices over his bride [you are lovely],
so will your God rejoice over you. (Is. 62:1–5, commentary added)

"But all who devour you will be devoured;
all your enemies will go into exile.
Those who plunder you will be plundered;
all who make spoil of you I will despoil.
But I will restore you to health and heal your wounds,"
declares the LORD,
"because you are called an outcast,
Zion for whom no one cares." (Jer. 30:16–17)

You really won't understand your life as a woman until you understand this:

You are passionately loved by the God of the universe.
You are passionately hated by his Enemy.

There is One greater than your Enemy. One who has sought you out from the beginning of time. God has come to heal your broken heart and restore your feminine soul.

- What does this section reveal regarding the enemy's fears about you?

- What do the verses from Isaiah and Jeremiah say about God's heart for you?

- According to today's reading, you really won't understand your life as a woman until you understand what two truths? Which is hardest for you to believe . . . and why?

CLOSING THOUGHTS

Take a deep breath. The truths in this session are critical for you to know in order for you to step into the more that Jesus has for you. There is more healing. More hope. More life. More goodness. And more freedom. It has all been won for you by your King, your Lord, and your Savior, Jesus Christ. He is victorious and in him, so are you. He has done everything and won everything so that you may have life in him and life to the full. And yes, you must play your part. If you want to pursue further reading on this subject—one good place to begin is Neil Andersons', "The Bondage Breaker". Bless you. Be encouraged. And stand firm.

SESSION FIVE

BEAUTY TO UNVEIL

"Beauty overwhelms us, enchants us, fascinates us, and calls us."

—Fr. Andrew Greeley

Welcome!

Welcome to Session Five of *Captivating*. If something stood out to you in your personal study, share briefly with your group.

Let's get started!

Core Scripture

Look up 1 Samuel 16:7 and write the second half of it in the space below.

Invite several women to read various translations of the passage aloud. Listen for fresh insights and share any thoughts about this verse with the group.

Watch the video segment for Session Five, streaming or on DVD. This summary is provided for your benefit as well as space to take additional notes.

Summary

Beauty is a difficult subject for women to talk about. Our desire for beauty has caused most of us countless tears and untold pain. Apart from God, beauty gets twisted, used and abused. And as we all know, the world's view of beauty is unattainable for the vast majority of women . . . and yet we long for it.

The Bible teaches that every woman is made in the image of God. Every woman bears his image in her heart and carries within her the very essence of Beauty.

Okay. Take a moment and let this sink in. You have a beauty all your own. You bear God's image and you are beautiful. Inside. And out. It is true.

This isn't about dresses and makeup. This is about our hearts—the very core of our being. We desire to possess a beauty that is worth pursuing, worth fighting for, a beauty that is core to who we truly are. We want beauty that can be seen yes but more a beauty that can be felt; a beauty that affects others; a beauty all our own to unveil.

The desire to be beautiful is an ageless longing. God has set eternity in our hearts. The longing to be beautiful is set there as well.

NOTES

GROUP DISCUSSION

Choose the questions that work best for your group.

1. What part of Stacey's story shed light on how we, as women, unveil our beauty?

2. Describe a beautiful moment you've had with another person. What made it so beautiful to you?

3. Describe a beautiful place that you love—and why.

4. How has beauty been defined for you in the past?

5. Though neither may be easy, is it easier for you to discuss your outer beauty or inner beauty? Why?

6. Do you believe beauty can increase with age? If so, can you share an example of this with the group?

7. We have a difficult time seeing our own beauty. Try this exercise. First, tell the woman next to you that she is beautiful. Next, try saying out loud "I am beautiful"? Which was harder to do? Why?

Closing Prayer

Leader or volunteer, close your group time in prayer:

> *Dear God,*
> *You are beautiful and I believe I bear your image. You know though that most days I don't feel very pretty, let alone beautiful. Would you please come to this place in my heart . . . this core place . . . and reveal to me my own beauty? Please heal the places in my heart that have been assaulted and hurt regarding beauty and establish your truth here. Would you tell me - Do you think I'm beautiful? How? Why? Please come for me, Jesus. It's in your name that I pray. Amen*

Recommended Reading

Before your group gathers for the next session, read Chapter 12 (*Your Irreplaceable Role)* in the book *Captivating*. Use the space provided to write any key points or questions you want to bring to the next group meeting.

BETWEEN-SESSIONS
PERSONAL STUDY

In this section, you're invited to further explore the material we've covered this week from *Captivating.* Each day offers a short reading from Chapter 8 (*Beauty to Unveil*) of John and Stasi's book—along with reflection questions designed to take you deeper into the themes of this week's study.

Journal or just jot a few thoughts after each question. At the start of the next session, there will be a few minutes to share any insights . . . but the primary goal of these questions is for your personal growth and private reflection.

DAY 1

THE ESSENCE OF A WOMAN

The essence of a woman is Beauty. She is meant to be the incarnation—our experience in human form—of a Captivating God. A God who *invites us.*

> Come, all you who are thirsty, come to the waters . . .
> Listen, listen to me, and eat what is good,
> and your soul will delight in the richest of fare. (Is. 55:1–2)

> You have stolen my heart, my sister, my bride;
> you have stolen my heart
> with one glance of your eyes,
> with one jewel of your necklace . . .
> You are a garden fountain,
> a well of flowing water
> streaming down from Lebanon. (Song 4:9, 15)

Beauty is what the world longs to experience from a woman. We know that. Somewhere down deep, we know it to be true. Most of our shame comes from this knowing and feeling that we have failed here. So listen to this: beauty is an essence that dwells in *every* woman. It was given to her by God. It was given to you.

Surely you would agree that God is nothing if not beautiful.

All around us God's creation shouts of his beauty and his goodness. The silhouette of lace on a barren tree draped with ice, the rays of sun streaming forth from a billowing cloud, the sound of a brook trickling over smooth stones, the form of a woman's body, and the face of a child anticipating the arrival of the ice-cream truck all speak of God's good heart if we will have but the eyes to see. The coming of spring after a hard winter is almost too glorious for a soul to bear. God's beauty is lavished on the world.

Beauty may be the most powerful thing on earth. Beauty *speaks*. Beauty *invites*. Beauty *nourishes*. Beauty *comforts*. Beauty *inspires*. Beauty is *transcendent*. Beauty draws us to God. As Simone Weil wrote, "The beauty of the world is almost the only way by which we can allow God to penetrate us . . . Beauty captivates the senses in order to obtain permission to pass straight through to the soul . . . The soul's inclination to love beauty is the trap God most frequently uses in order to win it."[3]

God has given this Beauty to Eve, to every woman. Beauty is core to a woman—who she is and what she longs to be—and one of the most glorious ways we bear the image of God in a broken and often ugly world. It's messy to talk about. It's mysterious. And that should not surprise us. Women are creatures of great mystery; not problems to be solved but mysteries to be enjoyed. And that, too, is part of her glory.

Women want to impact their world for good. As co-rulers with Adam, we are created to do so, and one of the key ways we influence our world is in making it a more beautiful place to live. We decorate our homes. We put flowers on the table. Pioneer women brought china teacups into the wilderness, and I bring a pretty tablecloth to eat on when my family camps. Some of us wear perfume, paint our toenails, color our hair, and pierce our ears, all in an effort to be ever more beautiful.

Beauty is the most *essential* and, yes, the most *misunderstood* of all the feminine qualities. We want you to hear clearly that it is an essence every woman carries from the moment of her creation. The only things standing in the way of our beauty are our doubts and fears, and the hiding and striving we fall to as a result.

- Have you ever considered that God is beautiful? Whether you have or this is a new thought, how would you describe God's beauty?

- Beauty is an essence that dwells in every woman, given to her by God. Are you aware of your beauty?

- "Women are creatures of great mystery; not problems to be solved but mysteries to be enjoyed." Do you identify with this statement in today's reading? Why or why not?

BEAUTY IS INVITING

Beauty beckons us. Beauty invites us. *Come, explore, immerse yourself.* God—Beauty himself—invites us to know him. "Taste and see that the Lord is good" (Ps. 34:8). He delights in alluring us and in revealing himself to those who wholeheartedly seek him. He wants to be known, to be explored. A woman does too. She fears it, but below the fear is a longing to be known, to be seen as beautiful and enjoyed. So the unveiled beauty of a woman entices and invites. The heart of the woman determines *what* it is she is inviting others *to*—to life or to death.

Proverbs speaks about two different women, two archetypes. One is Lady Folly; the other, Lady Wisdom. Both are lovely. Both set their tables with fine food and aged wine and dress in fine linens. Both call to the passersby to come in, taste, eat, linger. Lady Folly's door is the mouth of an open grave. Lady Wisdom's home is the passageway to discernment, holiness, and Life.

A woman who is striving invites others to strive. The message—sometimes implicit in her actions, sometimes explicit through her words—is, "Get your act together. Life is uncertain. There is no time for your heart here. Shape up. Get busy. That's what is important." She does not say, "All is well. All shall be well." Her fear doesn't allow it. She is withholding the very things her world needs.

By contrast a woman whose heart is at rest invites others to rest. We are invited to be ourselves. You find room for your soul. It expands. You can breathe again. You can rest. It is good. That is what it is like to be with a beautiful woman. You are free to be you. It is one of life's greatest gifts.

A woman who is unveiling her beauty is inviting others to life. She risks being vulnerable; exposing her true heart and inviting others to share theirs. She is not demanding, but she is hopeful. She offers her beauty by asking good questions and by bringing something of her times with God—an insight, a glimpse into his heart—to bear. She entices others to the heart of God.

You see, ultimately, a woman invites us to know God. To experience through her that God is merciful. That he is tender and kind. That God longs for us—to be known by us and to know us. She invites us to experience that God is good, deep, lovely, alluring. Captivating.

We know many of you are feeling, *But I'm not there. I'm not that kind of woman.* Here is where we "work out" our salvation as God works in us (Phil. 2:12–13). As you begin to live like this, you discover the places in your heart that still need the healing touch of Jesus. That's how it goes. We don't get to stay in hiding until we are whole; Jesus invites us to live as an inviting woman now, and find our healing along the way.

- Read Proverbs 9. How does Lady Wisdom reflect true beauty and Lady Folly represent false beauty?

- Would you describe yourself as a woman whose heart is at rest? Why or why not?

- Wherever you are on this journey, there is no shame. What places in your heart still need the healing touch of Jesus? Will you invite him to continue his work there?

DAY 3 OFFERING BEAUTY

For a woman to unveil her beauty means she is offering her heart. Not primarily her works or her usefulness (think Martha in the kitchen). Offering her *presence.* At family gatherings my mother hid in the kitchen. She cooked and baked and prepared and served and cleaned, and for the life of us, we couldn't get her out of there. We wanted her to share her life with us, her thoughts and her ideas, not just her efforts. She wouldn't come. And we were less because of it.

The gift of presence is a rare and beautiful gift. To come—unguarded, undistracted—and be fully present, fully engaged with whoever we are with at that moment. Have you noticed in reading the Gospels that people enjoyed being around Jesus? They wanted to be near him—to share a meal, take a walk, have a lingering conversation. It was the gift of his presence. When you were with him, you felt he was offering you his heart. When we offer our unguarded presence, we live like Jesus. And we invite others to do the same.

Beauty offers mercy. When my son Samuel was entering adolescence and leaving childhood behind, sometimes it was hard for me to let go. Sometimes his sullen attitude would make me mad. Boys-becoming-men are hard for a woman to understand. They act as if they don't need us anymore. Sometimes they act rudely in their emerging strength. When Sam acted that way, I would want to "come down" on him. (It always backfired when I did.) But that is not what he needed from me. He needed mercy. He needs it still. A kind word, a smile. Grace at the end of the day. When I would offer that to him, he would soften toward me, and our relationship would be recovered. A woman who is full of tender mercy and soft vulnerability is a powerful, lovely woman.

Beauty isn't demanding. Instead, it speaks from *desire*. When our children were young, John had to travel *a lot* for work. On his days off, he was pursuing a master's degree in counseling. That did not leave much time for our family. It fell to me to pay the bills, run the home, and parent the boys. Two of them were in Little League baseball; our youngest was still in diapers. I was busy. I was tired. I couldn't do it. I still remember the fear I felt when I asked John to sit down and talk. I told him that I couldn't do this family thing without him. I told him that I needed him. I asked for his help. I didn't demand him to come through. I didn't whine. I expressed my need and invited his strength, his presence. To my surprise, John told me that in my vulnerability to him, I had never been more feminine or more beautiful.

To offer your heart is to offer your desire—instead of your demand. Beauty offers desire.

- The gift of presence is a rare and beautiful gift. How do you think others would describe your presence? How do you experience Jesus' presence?

- Beauty offers mercy. How much tender mercy did you experience as a child? How much do you feel you are offering to others now?

- Do you feel you interact with those you love more from a place of desires or demands? How is this approach working for you?

DAY 4 CULTIVATING BEAUTY

Every woman possesses a captivating beauty. Every woman. But for most of us it has been long buried, wounded, and captive. It takes time for it to emerge into wholeness. It needs to be cultivated, restored, set free.

How do we cultivate beauty? How do we become ever more beautiful? By tending to our hearts with great care, as a master gardener tends to her work.

> My mother's sons were angry with me
> and made me take care of the vineyards;
> my own vineyard I have neglected. (Song 1:6)

Yes, life is harsh on a woman's heart. It has been hard on your heart. The assault on our beauty is real. But Jesus is urging us now to care for ourselves, watch over our hearts (Prov. 4:23). The world needs your beauty. That is why you are here. Your heart and your beauty are something to be treasured and nourished. And it takes time. Every gardener knows this. In our age of drive-throughs with the internet in the palm of our hands, we don't like to wait. But a newly planted rose's presentation in its first year is nothing compared to its second. If properly cared for, its second year's display doesn't hold a candle to its third. Gardens need to become established; their roots need to go deep through summer rains and winter frosts. A garden's beauty does not diminish with age; rather it takes years for it to become all that it can become.

Our hearts need to feed on beauty to sustain them. We need times of solitude and silence. We need times of refreshment and laughter and rest. We need to listen to the voice of God in our hearts as he tells us what we need. Sometimes it will be a bubble bath. Sometimes it is going for a walk in the woods, or taking a run or taking a nap. Often, Jesus will call us away to spend precious time alone with him. We grow in our intimacy with Jesus as we practice listening to his urging, his nudges within. Pay attention to them and follow. The Holy Spirit is our guide, our counselor, our comforter, our Great Friend, and he will lead us. Abiding in Christ means paying attention to the voice of God within, nourishing our own hearts and nourishing our relationship with him. Over time.

We have all heard it said that a woman is most beautiful when she is in love. It's true. You've seen it yourself. When a woman knows that she is loved and loved deeply, she glows from the inside. This radiance stems from a heart that has had its deepest questions answered. *Am I lovely? Am I worth fighting for? Have I been and will I continue to be romanced?* When these questions are answered yes, a restful, quiet spirit settles in a woman's heart.

And every woman can have these questions answered yes. You have been and you will continue to be romanced all your life. Yes. Our God finds you lovely. Jesus has moved heaven and earth to win you for himself. He will not rest until you are completely his. The King is enthralled by your beauty. He finds you captivating.

Beauty is a quality of the soul that expresses itself in the visible world. You can see it. You can touch it. You are drawn to it. Beauty illuminates. Its essence, says Thomas Aquinas, is its "luminosity." It is bound up with the immortal. Beauty flows from a heart that is alive. We have known women you might describe as "frumpy," who seemed to care nothing for their appearance. We have seen them become women who possessed great beauty. We watched it grow in them as they discovered that they were deeply loved, as their hearts came alive in response to the Great Romancer. We *are* romanced. We are loved. When we *are* at rest in that knowledge, we can offer our hearts to others and invite them to Life.

- In what ways do you—or would you like to—intentionally cultivate beauty in your life?

- Write Proverbs 4:23 in the space below. What do you think it means to nurture or watch over your heart? Why do you believe we're instructed to do this above all else?

- God is enthralled by your beauty. Is that easy or hard for you to believe? Why?

DAY 5

FAITH, HOPE, AND LOVE

Unveiling our beauty really just means unveiling our feminine hearts.

It's scary, for sure. That is why it is our greatest expression of faith, because we are going to have to trust Jesus—really trust him. We'll have to trust him that we *have* a beauty, that what he has said of us is true. And we'll have to trust him with how it goes when we offer it, because that is out of our control. We'll have to trust him when it hurts, and we'll have to trust him when we are finally seen and enjoyed. That's why unveiling our beauty is *how* we live by faith.

Unveiling our beauty is our greatest expression of hope. We hope that it will matter, that our beauty really does make a difference. We hope there is a greater and higher Beauty, hope we are reflecting that Beauty, and hope it will triumph. Our hope is that all is well because of Jesus and that all will be well because of him. So we unveil beauty in hope. And finally, we unveil beauty in the hope that Jesus is *growing* our beauty. Yes, we are not yet what we long to be. But we are underway. Restoration has begun. To offer beauty now is an expression of hope that it will be completed.

And unveiling beauty is our greatest expression of love, because it is what the world most needs from us. When we choose not to hide, when we choose to offer our hearts, we are choosing to love. Jesus offers; he invites; he is present. That is how he loves. That is how we love—sincerely, as the Scripture says, "from the heart" (1 Peter 1:22). Our focus shifts from self-protection to the hearts of others. We offer Beauty so that their hearts might come alive, be healed, know God. That is love.

- Why do you think letting our beauty be seen by the world is scary?

- What are several ways the unveiling of our beauty expresses hope?

- How does the unveiling of your beauty uniquely reveal love to this hurting world?

CLOSING THOUGHTS

A beautiful woman is a woman whose heart is alive—or better—who is increasingly becoming more alive. Christ has come that we might have life and life to the full. (John 10:10b) It is his desire for you. His desire also includes that you rest in the truth that you are loved. Right now, you are totally loved. When we believe we are loved in the moment—rather than believe that we have to work in order to become loved—something in our heart settles. Remain in that posture for a while, meditating on the truth that you are loved—and you become a woman whose heart is both at rest and alive. Alive in the love of God—and responding to being loved by loving God in return. And there is nothing more beautiful in a woman than that.

SESSON SIX

YOUR IRREPLACEABLE ROLE

Mary responded, "I am the Lord's servant.
May everything you have said come true."
—**Luke 1:38 NLT**

Welcome!

Congratulations! This is the last group gathering—Session Six—of our *Captivating* study. We hope this has been a rich time for you and we're so happy that you have gone on this journey. Spend a few minutes sharing where your heart has been restored so far.

Now, with much joy, let's get started with our final session!

Core Scripture

Look up Genesis 1:28 and write it in the space below.

Invite several women to read various translations of the passage aloud. Listen for fresh insights and share any thoughts about this verse with the group.

VIDEO

Watch the video segment for Session Six, streaming or on DVD. This summary is provided for your benefit as well as space to take additional notes.

Summary

A woman doesn't come alive being merely useful. We want our lives to matter and to matter deeply. We want to be needed. Irreplaceable. And so does our God. It is in fact, right here, in this core desire of our heart, that we bear His image.

Women are wired to play their irreplaceable role in a heroic adventure that is shared. It's a spiritual longing—one bestowed upon us at our creation—it runs deep in our bones, our souls, our hearts. The ways it plays out is as varied as the women who exist but this core desire of our hearts to be irreplaceable and essential is one that we all share. As we grow in Christ and become more and more his, more healed and more truly ourselves, God recovers and restores our desires. And if we never have been aware of any, he awakens them.

If you don't know what your irreplaceable role is, what God has written on your heart? Think again of what you dreamt of when you were young. Another clue to discover your irreplaceable role is the way you have been wounded in your life. What has been assaulted? What lies have been spoken to you? These wounds often reveal the secret of your glory and what you are meant to bring to the world. Why else would you be so attacked there?

Ask God to reveal to you the ways you are living out in partnership with him bringing his Kingdom to bear on a hurting world today. It may not look as sparkly and shiny as you think it should but the Kingdom of God is lived out in the nitty gritty ins and outs of daily life.

All women have an irreplaceable role to play and are called to be life-givers. Remember, you are an *ezer kenegdo*. The way we live this out expresses itself in a myriad of ways throughout our lives. Some of the desires that God has written on our heart are specific and some are mythic. You are a woman. You are a life-giver. You do have an irreplaceable role to play. We need you. God needs you. Choose him. First. Last. And in between.

GROUP DISCUSSION

Choose the questions that work best for your group.

1. How did Cherie's story expand your understanding of what it means to be irreplaceable?

2. What was evoked for you during this session?

3. Is the fact that the Genesis 1:28 mandate to have a fierce mastery over the earth was given to both men and women together a surprise to you? What does it mean to you personally?

4. If you could do anything, what would it be? How long have you had this dream? And who else would be involved in this heroic adventure?

5. Do you believe you are needed? Why or why not?

6. Who would you like to impact most for the Kingdom of God? Share more about what led you to choose this person.

7. One of the best ways you can fix your gaze on Jesus to spend time worshipping him. What particular worship song helps you focus your eyes on Jesus . . . and why?

Closing Prayer

Leader or volunteer, close your group time in prayer:

My dear Jesus,
I would love to have an irreplaceable role to play in a shared heroic adventure. Some days, though, that just feels ridiculously out of reach. But Lord,you look at both me and my life much differently than I do. I pray to see as you do and to embrace the way you see. I pray for the courage to awaken to the desires you have placed in my life and to step into them with you in a divine partnership. You have my yes, Lord. You have my life. You have my love. In Jesus' Name. Amen.

BETWEEN-SESSIONS
PERSONAL STUDY

In this section, you're invited to further explore the material we've covered this week from *Captivating*. Each day offers a short reading from Chapter 12 of John and Stasi's book—along with reflection questions designed to take you deeper into the themes of this week's study.

Journal or just jot a few thoughts after each question. As always, the primary goal of these questions is for your personal growth and private reflection.

DAY 1

THE POWER OF A WOMAN'S LIFE

When the history of the world is finally told rightly—one of the great joys when we reach the Wedding Feast of the Lamb—it will be as clear as day that women have been essential to every great move of God upon this earth.

I wanted to say "*nearly* every great move," not wanting to overstate a crucial point and recognizing that there are moments when men have led the way. But Stasi chimed in and said, "Those men had mothers, didn't they?!" I was thinking of Moses who seemed to lead the Exodus, but it quickly dawned on me that it was his mother who saved his life as a baby (at the risk of her own life and the lives of her entire family). It was his sister who stayed with the babe and suggested a nursemaid when Pharaoh's daughter took him for her own. (That nurse would be, of course, his mother.) Okay. I concede. Women have been essential to every great movement of God.

Certainly there are those amazing moments in the Old Testament like the story of Rahab, who secured the Hebrews' successful military launch into the Promised Land.

And Esther, who saved her people from genocide and secured the future of Israel . . . and of the world. It's clear that women supported the ministry of Jesus, financially and emotionally, and women were the ones who stayed with him when nearly all the men hightailed it and ran. As we read the story of the spreading gospel and the birth of the church in the New Testament, we encounter women like Lydia, whose home became the staging point for the evangelism of Thyatira and Philippi; women like Nympha and Apphia, who hosted the emerging church in their homes—again, at great risk to themselves and their loved ones. There is Priscilla, who risked her life to help Paul spread the gospel, and Junias, who was with Paul when he was in prison and whom he called "outstanding among the apostles" (Rom. 16:7).

And of course, the salvation of mankind rested on the courage of a woman, a teenage girl. What if she had said no? What if any of them had said no?

To try and give honor to women in the sweep of history is impossible here. It would be easier to think of any of the great or small turning points in God's rescue of mankind and try to find one where women were not irreplaceable. From the beginning, Eve was God's gift to the world—his ezer kenegdo for us. History is still unfolding, and your existence on this earth as a woman is proof that you have an irreplaceable role to play. You are a woman, are you not? An ezer kenegdo to your core. Your lingering disbelief (may it be fading away) that anything important hangs on your life is only evidence of the long assault on your heart by the one who knows who you could be and fears you.

There is much life-saving that needs to be done yet, and someone needs to do it. Not in a pressure-filled, *You'd better get to it* kind of a way. Rather, an invitation. Your feminine heart is an invitation by your Creator. To what? To play an irreplaceable role in his Story. Isn't that what your Lover wrote there? Some dream, some desire, something so core to who you are it almost hurts to think of it. The very longing is such a part of your being it's scary even to give it a voice. You may not know the dream itself yet. But you know the *longing* to play an irreplaceable part. That is a good beginning.

Ezer is woven into the fabric of your feminine heart. You must live this out. What lives, what destinies are hanging on *your* yes to God?

- What is your reaction to the statement that women have been essential to every great movement of God?

- Which story from Scripture are you most to drawn to as an illustration of the irreplacable role women have played in the history of our faith? Why?

- What unique longing has God woven into the fabric of your feminine heart?

DAY 2

WHAT IS WRITTEN ON YOUR HEART?

As I said earlier, the invitations of Jesus come to us in many ways.

Sometimes they come through a circumstance, an opportunity that opens before us. Sometimes they come through other people who see something in us that we may not yet see, and they invite us to step forth in some way. But God's invitations ultimately are matters of the heart. They come through our passions, those desires set deep within us. What is it you yearn to see happen—how do you long for the world to be a better place? What makes you so angry you nearly see red? What brings you to tears?

You will find that as God restores your heart and sets you free, you will recover long-lost passions, long-forsaken dreams. You'll find yourself drawn to some vision for making the world a better place.

Those emerging desires are invitations—not to rush out and attempt them immediately. That also is naive. They are invitations to bring your heart to your Lover and ask him to clarify, to deepen, to speak to you about how and when and with whom.

We love Frederick Buechner's description when he writes, "The place that God calls us is that place where the world's deep hunger and our deep desire meet."

- How do you yearn to make the world a better place?

- Have you considered that God has given you this passion? How does seeing it as his invitation shape your sense of having an irreplaceable role in a great adventure?

- Frederick Buechner says, "The place that God calls us is that place where the world's deep hunger and our deep desire meet." How might this play out in your life . . . and how would the world be different because of it?

DAY 3
DO NOT GIVE WAY TO FEAR

Of course this is scary.

Responding to the invitations of Jesus often feels like the riskiest thing we've ever done. Just ask Rahab, Esther, Ruth, and Mary. Ask Jeanine, Ellie, Tammy, Carol, and Kathleen. Webster defines *risk* as exposing one's life to the possibility of injury, damage, or loss. The life of the friends of God is a life of profound risk. The risk of loving others. The risk of stepping out and offering, speaking up and following our

God-given dreams. The risk of playing the irreplaceable role that is ours to play. Of course it is hard. If it were easy, you'd see lots of women living this way.

So let's come back then to what Peter said when he urged women to offer their beauty to others in love. This is the secret of femininity unleashed:

> Do not give way to fear. (1 Peter 3:6)

The reason we fear to step out is because we know that it might not go well (is that an understatement?). We have a history of wounds screaming at us to play it safe. We feel so deeply that if it doesn't go well, if we are not received well, their reaction becomes the verdict on our lives, on our very beings, on our hearts. We fear that our deepest doubts about ourselves as women will be confirmed. Again. That we will hear yet again the message of our wounds, the piercing negative answers to our Question. That is why we can *only* risk stepping out when we are resting in the love of God. When we have received his verdict on our lives—that we are chosen and dearly loved. That he finds us captivating. Then we are free to offer.

You could say that people did not respond very well to Jesus' love, to his stepping out in faith and playing the role that was his alone to play. And that would be a ridiculous understatement. The very people that Jesus died for hurled insults at him, mocked him, spat at him, crucified him. Jesus had to trust his Father *profoundly*, with his very being. Peter uses him as our example saying, "Follow in his steps . . . He did not retaliate when he was insulted. When he suffered, he did not threaten to get even. He left his case in the hands of God" (1 Peter 2:21–23 NLT). Or, as another translation has it, "he entrusted himself" to God. He was okay. He entrusted himself to God.

A few verses later Peter, writing to women, says, "In the same way . . . do not give way to fear" (3:1, 6). Jesus lived a life of love, and he invites us to do the same. Regardless of the response.

It was very hard and immensely risky for me to begin to speak and offer from my heart at our women's retreats. Terrifying, really. You see, when I first began to speak, I was severely overweight and struggle here still. My sin, my addiction, was plain for all to see. To stand in front of a group of women and be clearly failing in the outward beauty department was humbling and hard. It has felt risky for me to write this book with John. Risky to share so much of my story. Risky because I'm a first-time author and he is so well-known, so good at it.

But we don't get to wait to offer our lives until we have our acts together. We don't get that luxury. If we did, would anyone *ever* feel like offering *anything*? God asks us to be vulnerable. He invites us to share and give in our weaknesses. He wants us to offer the beauty that he has given us even when we are keenly aware that it is not all that we wish it were. He wants us to *trust* him.

How it turns out is no longer the point. Living in this way, as a woman alive, is a choice we make because it is the woman we want to be. It is our loving response to our Lover's invitation.

- In what areas does fear most trouble your heart?

- Write 1 Peter 3:6 below. Do you see these words as a hopeful possibility or a tangible reality for followers of Jesus?

- God invites us to offer the beauty he's given us—even when we feel it isn't what we wish it was. How does it feel to step into this inviation now rather than wait until we feel we have our act together or are more qualified?

DAY 4
BE PRESENT

To live as an authentic, ransomed, and redeemed woman means to be real and present in this moment. If we continue to hide, much will be lost. We cannot have intimacy with God or anyone else if we stay hidden and offer only who we think we ought to be or what we believe is wanted. We cannot play the ezer role we were meant to play if we remain bound by shame and fear, presenting only to the world the face we have learned is safe. *You have only one life to live. It would be best to live your own.*

What have we to offer, really, other than who we are and what God has been pouring into our lives? It was not by accident that you were born; it was not by chance that you have the desires you do. The Victorious Trinity has planned on your being here now, "for such a time as this" (Est. 4:14). We need you.

> Jesus knew that the Father had put all things under his power, *and that he had come from God and was returning to God*; so he got up from the meal, took off his outer clothing, and wrapped a towel around his waist. After that, he poured water into a basin and began to wash his disciples' feet, drying them with the towel that was wrapped around him. (John 13:3–5, emphasis added)

Jesus knew who he was. He knew where he had come from and where he was going. He knew why he was here. And so, in power and strength, in humility and complete freedom, he offers. He ministers to us and ultimately he pours out his life as an offering for ours. Pleasing and holy and acceptable. Jesus does this, he says, as "an example that you should do as I have done for you" (John 13:15).

God really does want you to know who you are. He wants you to be able to understand the story of your life, to know where you have come from, and to know where you are going. There is freedom there. Freedom to be and to offer and to love. So, may we take a moment and remind you who you truly are?

You are a woman. An image bearer of God. The Crown of Creation. You were chosen before time and space, and you are wholly and dearly loved. You are sought after, pursued, romanced, the passionate desire of your fiancé, Jesus. You are dangerous in your beauty and your life-giving power. And you are needed.

As a woman who has been ransomed and redeemed, you can be strong and tender. You speak to the world of God's mercy, mystery, beauty, and his desire for intimate relationship. You are inviting; you can risk being vulnerable, offering the weight of your life as well as your need for more because you are safe in God's love. You labor with God to bring forth life—in creativity, in work, in others. Your aching, awakened heart leads you to the feet of Jesus, where you wait *on* him and wait *for* him. The eyes of his heart are ever upon you. The King is captivated by your beauty.

We need you. We need you to awaken to God more fully and to awaken to the desires of the heart that he placed within you so that you will come alive to him and to the role that is yours to play. Perhaps you are meant to be a concert musician or a teacher. Perhaps you are meant to be a neurologist or a horse trainer. Perhaps you are to be an activist for ecology or the poor or the aged or the ill. You are certainly called to be a woman, wherever else he leads you.

And that is crucial, dear heart. Whatever your particular calling, you are meant to grace the world with your dance, to follow the lead of Jesus wherever he leads you.

He will lead you first into himself; and then, with him, he will lead you into the world that he loves and needs you to love.

It is by Invitation.

- How does it help to remember—no matter how crazy this world becomes—that God put you here "for such a time as this"? (Est. 4:14)

- You were chosen before time and space. You are needed. You have a role that is yours alone to play. What do those thoughts stir in you?

- What has been holding you back from your destiny? Write a prayer below asking God to help fully awaken the desires of your heart.

DAY 5

TAKE MY HAND

There is a scene near the end of the film *Anna and the King* I wish I could now play for you. Let me describe it.

The setting is nineteenth-century Siam, a tiny but beautiful Asian country still in the grips of its ancient past. Anna, an English woman living in Siam as a tutor to the king's many offspring, has helped King Mangkut prepare for a state dinner. He wants to show the British that his country is ready to enter into the affairs of the world, so the dinner is given in the English style—silverware, tablecloths, candlelight, and, at the end of the meal, ballroom dancing.

When the feast is over and it comes time for the first dance, the king stands and extends his hand to Anna. He invites her to dance with him. He fixes his gaze upon her and is distracted by nothing and no one else. He waits for her response. She is clearly surprised, taken aback, but has the grace to respond and stand. As they walk past the long table, the king's eyes never stray from hers, a smile playing on his lips. Others are upset that he has chosen her. Some watch with contempt, others with pleasure. It is of no consequence to the king or to Anna.

Anna came to the ball prepared. She was beautiful in a striking gown that shimmered like starlight. She spent hours getting herself ready—her hair, her dress, her heart. As they reach the dance floor, Anna expresses her fear of dancing with the king before the eyes of others. "We wouldn't want to end up in a heap," she says. His answer to her questioning heart? "I am King. I will lead."

Jesus is extending his hand to you. He is inviting you to dance with him. He asks, "May I have this dance . . . every day of your life?" His gaze is fixed on you. He is captivated by your beauty. He is smiling. He cares nothing of the opinion of others. He is standing. He will lead. He waits for your response.

> My lover spoke and said to me,
> "Arise, my darling,
> my beautiful one,
> and come with me." (Song 2:10)

- What most stands out to you about this scene from *Anna and the King*? Why?

- In the film, Anna expresses her fear of dancing with the King in front of others. Does the thought of dancing with Jesus provoke any fear in you? If so, can you name what it is?

- Write Song 2:10 in your own words below. What is your favorite part of this intimate invitation? Are you ready to accept it?

CLOSING THOUGHTS

Bless you friend! Bless you. You have done good work here with our God diving into the treasures of your beautiful heart. Well done you. In the end, the greatest treasure in the universe is Jesus. To know him is to love him. Oh, may we all continue to grow in knowing him more deeply and responding to his love in kind. Living our lives with him is the grandest adventure of all! And know, that no matter how far we have traveled on our journeys, there is always more goodness to be had. There is so much more to discover about the heart of Jesus. There is so much more healing and life and love for us to discover in him. Let's press on together for the more he has for us.

We'd love to have you join us at WildatHeart.org to contine the journey!

LEADER'S GUIDE

Thank you for your willingness to lead your group through *Captivating: Unveiling the Mystery of a Woman's Soul.* The rewards of leading are different from the rewards of participating, and we hope you find your own walk with Jesus deepened by this experience. This leader's guide will give you some tips on how to prepare for your time together and facilitate a meaningful experience for your group members.

What Does It Take to Lead This Study?

Get together and watch God show up. This is the beauty of how a small group works. Gather several women together who have a hunger for God, who long to be known and seen, and are willing to be open and honest with God and themselves. The Lord will honor this every time and show up in the group. You don't have to be a pastor, priest, theologian, or counselor to lead a group through this study. Just invite your sisters over, watch the video, and talk about it. All you need is a willing heart, a little courage, and God will do the rest.

How This Study Works

As the group leader, you will want to make sure everyone in your group has a copy of this study guide. (The group members will also want to have a copy of the *Captivating* book if they are doing the recommended readings for each session.) It works best if you can get the guides (and books) to your group *before* the first meeting. That way, everyone can read the material in the book ahead of time and be prepared to watch the first video session together.

This series is presented in six video sessions, with each session being approximately fifteen to twenty minutes in length. Each week, you will meet together to watch the video and discuss the session. This series can also be used in classroom settings, such as Sunday school classes, though you may need to modify the discussion time depending on the size of the class. You could even use the video as sessions for a special prayer retreat.

Basically, each week you will: (1) discuss the opening Core Scripture questions, (2) watch the video sessions, (3) talk about them, and then (4) reflect on what you have learned by completing the between-sessions activities. That's it!

A Few Tips for Leading a Group

The setting really matters. If you can choose to meet in a living room over a conference room in a church, do it. Pick an environment that's conducive to people relaxing and getting real. Remember the enemy likes to distract us when it comes to seeking God, so do what you can to remove these obstacles from your group (silence cell phones, limit background noise, no texting). Set the chairs or couches in a circle to prevent having a "classroom" feel.

Have some refreshments! Coffee and water will do; cookies and snacks are even better. Everyone tends to be nervous when they join a new group, so if you can give them something to hold onto (like a warm mug of coffee), they will relax a lot more. It's human nature.

Good equipment is important. Meet where you can watch the video sessions on a screen big enough for everyone to see and enjoy. Get or borrow the best gear you can. Also, be sure to test your media equipment ahead of time to make sure everything is in working condition. This way, if something isn't working, you can fix it or make other arrangements before the meeting begins. (You'll be amazed at how the enemy will try to mess things up for you!)

Be honest. Remember that your honesty will set the tone for your time together. Be willing to answer questions personally, as this will set the pace for the length of your group members' responses and will make others more comfortable in sharing.

Stick to the schedule. Strive to begin and end at the same time each week. The women in your group are busy, and if they can trust you to be a good steward of their time, they will be more willing to come back each week. Of course, you want to be open to the work God is doing, and at times you may want to *linger* in prayer or discussion. Remember the clock serves *you;* your group doesn't serve the clock. But work to respect the group's time, especially when it comes to limiting the discussion times.

Don't be afraid of silence or emotion. Welcome awkward moments. The material presented during this study will challenge the group members to reconsider some of their beliefs and compel them to make the necessary changes in their lives. Don't be afraid to ease into the material with the group.

Create space for the group to share. You're both the leader and a member of this small group. They will follow your lead, so assure the group that everyone will have time to share and set the example for not having anyone dominate the conversation.

Prepare for your meeting. Watch the video for the meeting ahead of time. Although it may feel a bit like cheating because you'll know what's coming, you will be better prepared for what the session might stir in the hearts of your group members. Also be sure to review the material in this guide and spend some time in prayer. In fact, the *most important* thing you can do is simply pray ahead of time each week:

> *Lord Jesus, come and rule this time. Let your Spirit fill this place. Bring your kingdom here. Take us right to the things we really need to talk about and rescue us from every distraction. Show us the heart of the Father. Meet each woman here. Give us your grace and love for one another. In your name I pray.*

Make sure your group members are prepared. Before the first meeting, secure enough copies of the study guide for each member. Have these ready and on hand for the first meeting, or make sure the participants have purchased them. Send out a reminder email or a text a couple of days before the meeting to make sure folks don't forget about it.

As You Gather

You will find the following counsel to be especially helpful when you meet for the first time as a group. I offer these comments in the spirit of "here is what I would do if I were leading a group through this study."

First, as the group gathers, start your time with introductions if people don't know each other. Begin with yourself and share your name, if you have a spouse and/or children, how you spend your days, and what you want to learn most from this study. Going first will put the group more at ease.

After the introductions, go through the Core Scripture section as you have time. Then jump right into watching the video teaching, as this will help get things started on a strong note. In the following weeks, you may want to start by allowing folks to catch up a little with some "how are you?" kind of banter. Too much of this burns up your meeting time, but you have to allow some room for it because it helps build relationships among the group members.

Note that each group will have its own personality and dynamics. Typically, people will hold back the first week or two until they feel the group is "safe." Then they will begin to share. Again, don't let it throw you if your group seems a bit awkward at first. Of course, some people *never* want to talk, so you'll need to coax them out as time goes on. But let it go the first week.

Insight for Discussion

If the group members are in any way open to talking about their lives as it relates to this material, you will likely *not* have enough time for every question suggested in this study guide. That's okay! Pick the questions ahead of time that you know you definitely want to cover, just in case you end up only having time to discuss a few of them.

You set the tone for the group. Your honesty and vulnerability during discussion times will tell them what they can share. How *long* you talk will give them an example of how long they should respond. Give some thought to what stories or insights from your own work in the study guide you want to highlight.

A Final Note. The greatest temptation for most small group leaders is to add to the video teaching with a little "teaching session" of their own. Even though you have much wisdom to add, this is unhelpful for three reasons:

1. The discussion time will be the richest time during your meeting. The video sessions have been intentionally kept short so you can have plenty of time for discussion. If you add to the teaching, you sacrifice this precious time.

2. You don't want your group members *teaching, lecturing,* or *correcting* one another. The group members are all at a different place in their spiritual journey. If you

set a tone by teaching, the group will feel like they have the freedom to teach one another. That can be disastrous for group dynamics.

3. The participants will be watching the video teachings during your group time and exploring the topics covered in more detail by completing the between-sessions activities. They don't need more content! What they want is a chance to talk and process their own lives in light of all they have taken in.

A Strong Close

Some of the best learning times will take place after the group time as God brings new insights to the participants during the week. Encourage group members to write down any questions they have as work through the between-sessions exercises. Make sure they know you are available for them as they explore the material. Finally, make sure you close your time by praying together—either by following the suggested prompts or coming up with your own closing prayers. Ask two or three people to pray, inviting God to fill your group and lead each person during this study.

Thank you again for taking the time to lead your group. May this study help restore our feminine hearts and reveal the glorious design that God originally intended for us as women.

ENDNOTES

1. UK Border Agency; Country of Origin Information Service, "Country of Origin Information Report—Democratic Republic of the Congo," *United Kingdom: Home Office* (27 January 2009), https://www.refworld.org/docid/498166df2.html.
2. *The Lord of the Rings: The Two Towers*, directed by Peter Jackson (New York: New Line Cinema and WingNut Films, 2009).
3. Simone Weil, "Love of the Order of the World," in *Waiting for God*, trans. Emma Craufurd (New York: Routledge, (1951, 2010), 101.

Complete the Journey Into the Heart of a Woman

About Stasi Eldredge

Stasi Eldredge is a *New York Times* bestselling author, and her books have sold nearly 3 million copies and changed women's lives all over the world. A teacher and conference speaker, Stasi is the cofounder of Wild at Heart, a ministry devoted to helping people discover the heart of God, recover their own hearts in God's love, and learn to live in God's Kingdom. Her passion is to see lives transformed by the beauty of the gospel. She and her husband, John, make their home in Colorado Springs, Colorado.